CHURCH WORK WITH YOUNG PEOPLE

CHURCH WORK WITH YOUNG PEOPLE

HARRY THOMAS STOCK

THE PILGRIM PRESS
BOSTON CHICAGO

PRINTED IN THE UNITED STATES OF AMERICA
THE PLIMPTON PRESS · NORWOOD · MASS.

THE PURPOSE OF THIS BOOK

THIS volume is intended primarily for pastors, directors of religious education, superintendents of church schools, class teachers, counselors and leaders of societies and clubs, and members of committees on religious education. It is written with the opportunities and problems of the local church and community in mind. Its main purpose is to assist responsible leaders in developing a program of Christian education which will be adequate to the needs of modern youth.

The young people themselves — as adolescents and future adults — are our chief interest. Organization, methods and materials are for the purpose of making possible the richest human experience — an experience which has that abundance of which Jesus spoke. The book may, therefore, be said to be "pupil-centered." But the young people are never to be thought of as solitary beings; religious education must deal with growing persons in the totality of their relationships, human and divine.

From another angle, the volume may be called "church-centered," but only in the sense that the church is recognized to be the agency (next to the home) which must bear the primary responsibility for religious education. Mindful of the character-building processes fostered by the public schools and by community agencies of a semi-religious character, the author maintains that the churches (individually and in coöperation) must initiate and develop a comprehensive program of religious education. For we are committed to objectives which are distinctly Christian. Christian homes and Christian churches cannot shift the responsibility in this field to organizations engaged in moral education, useful though their activities may be.

The author prefers not to be labelled as belonging to any particular school of educational theory. He wants to be thought of as being Christian in his purpose and educational in his method. He has no set of organizational or methodological ideas which he wishes to "sell." He abhors bondage to organizations, curricular systems, educational notions, ancient traditions, modern fads. He believes in freedom, and is convinced that Christianity brings the greater liberty and that education is a process by which youth is enabled to flower into the fulness of personality. But he thinks it is bad education and worse religion to encourage young people to grow Topsy-like, without constructive guidance.

If there is one educational idea for which the book may be thought to be propaganda, it is this: programs of religious education must be cut to measure. Systems nicely ordered in secretarial offices, theories which emerge out of sequestered study unrelated to the processes of social life, programs of "canned goods" recommended as containing the vitamines of Christian character — these have too often been instruments of paralysis rather than life-giving aids. The only program which will prove adequate for a local group is one which begins with a study of the specific situation and which uses competent help from all available sources. This, then, is the text upon which the volume is based: the first step in any local program of religious education is that the local leadership shall build that program itself, after a careful study of needs and opportunities. The pages which follow contain principles, procedures, concrete plans which may help the local leaders in building wisely and courageously a program of church work which shall have its fruitage in Christian character.

H. T. S.

CONTENTS

APPENDIX

Chapter I

OBJECTIVES IN YOUNG PEOPLE'S WORK

AMERICAN Protestantism is genuinely interested in young people. During the last century it has given hearty support to the Sunday school movement and to the young people's society. Within recent years it has welcomed the expanded conception of religious education and has tried to adapt its program to meet the new demands. There are, to be sure, apathy and inefficiency at many points, but signs of enthusiastic interest are widespread: the extension of the program through the weekday schools, the rapid development of summer conferences, new buildings to house the church school, the strengthening of the staffs of national departments of young people's work, the generous support given to extra-church agencies committed to programs of moral education. If the church has failed to function efficiently, it must at least be given credit for a desire to serve its youth and for an enlarging appreciation of its opportunity and responsibility.

The present status of young people's work is decidedly hopeful. Notable gains in membership are reported. A new quality is evident in the work of classes and societies. Purposes and processes are being analyzed, evaluated and modified with the intent that a truly Christian generation may be produced. Trained minds are revising old plans in the light of the new knowledge gained through the physical and social sciences, and of the findings of modern pedagogy. The church not only approves this spirit of research and experiment but eagerly grasps at every idea which will help to make effective its work.

A new sense of responsibility has come to local leaders. The task of being a teacher or counselor is recognized as one worthy of the best talents and the devotion of the most competent adults. Religious education is seen to be a local task — in both the formulation and execution of programs — and a new creativity is apparent within churches of all denominations. It is also a community responsibility, and a larger degree of coöperation among communions is one of the outstanding signs of the times. This local coöperation is matched by the national boards of religious education, almost all of which are united in fellowship, research, and certain program activities. In the midst of universal concern for the future of the race and of confusion regarding methods of procedure, there is a real determination on the part of Protestant leaders to find the best way and to be of the greatest service to the growing generation. This zeal in seeking to improve the local program, so that it will produce the best results in character, is the most significant fact in present-day religious education.

Formulating Objectives

Countless innovations are being tried. The church is frankly in an era of experimentation. There will always be need of further experimentation, but there is a growing conviction that we need to synthesize some of the findings of our investigations and experiences. While the dominant mood is one of impatience with national systems of religious education and superimposed programs of young people's work, it is recognized that some kind of purposive policy is needed if the successive units of a curriculum are to contribute cumulatively to Christian character. Committees of religious education are consequently facing the underlying issue, "What is the purpose of religious education?" Leaders who are responsible for young people's work cannot make much progress until they have found an answer to the question, "What objectives should determine our program?"

Such objectives must be formulated in the light of human need. Experts are diligently studying the range of adolescent interests and problems; the wise leader will avail himself of their conclusions. But he will also make his own study of the particular young people in his parish, who are subject to the peculiar environment of his community. Some needs are universal, others grow out of local situations. Some are distinctly personal, others are shared by the group. Some are apparent to young people, others are not recognized and must be stimulated by wise leadership. Some have to do with the present, others will not arise until the years of maturity. Through such facts as the scholars are able to disclose and through unending study by local leaders, the needs of youth must be clearly understood before a series of adequate objectives can be outlined. After such objectives have been agreed upon, materials and methods and organization will be modified so as to make a program truly effective in achieving the desired goals.

It is, therefore, urged that the responsible committee in the church set for itself the task of determining the objectives for its adolescent departments, spending as long a time as may be necessary upon the project. Having done this, they are ready to study the type of curriculum needed, and to consider what materials and methods will be the best instruments for accomplishing the intended results. In any such survey the entire teaching force of the young people's division should join.

The young people themselves may be asked to formulate a statement of the chief contributions which they believe the church should make to their widening experience. This they will do eagerly and with pointed results, if they understand the purposes of the study. Such a project would furnish the basis of fully a quarter's work in the young people's classes or society. It would probably suggest, also, the immediate future activity for these adolescent groups. Together, old and young should come to a definite understanding of just what the church program should try to accomplish. Adequate organization, suitable materials, effective methods — these wait upon this basic study of needs and objectives.

The suggestions which form the content of this chapter may be used as supplementary material for such a survey. They may provoke the consideration of certain issues not apparent to local leaders. But the objectives finally chosen as the basis for the local program of religious education should be the product of the thoughtful study of the group itself. Such a study must begin with the needs of the young people — individual and collective, present and future — both such as represent the yearnings of youth and those which ought to be stimulated within the adolescent mind.

The Growing Life of Youth

Life-habits are determined early. Adult viewpoints are being established during the teens. The process of religious education concerns itself, of necessity, both with the present experience of young people and with the demands which adulthood will make upon them. Some of the objectives for a program of religious education will relate themselves largely to the immediate present, others apply chiefly to the future. But the process is one: as we succeed in meeting the requirements of the day we shall contribute to a wise and useful mature life, and it is impossible to meet the issues of the present satisfactorily without taking into account the experiences which are certain to come with later years.

At least the following opportunities are presented to the church as it faces its duty toward the youth of the parish:

1. To help young people to understand the nature of religion and the meaning of Christianity. The Christian church is committed to the belief that religion is essential to the highest type of life. It has the duty, therefore, of enabling young people to lay hold upon that religion which will give the richest quality to human experience, and of making it possible for them to share this experience with others.

Most young people believe in God. But the picture is hazy, the conception vague. God exists for them as a necessary idea inherited from the past. In too few cases have they that appreciative and discerning attitude whereby he has become the significant reality behind every material creation, the beneficent spirit within every joyful relationship. True, the word " love " is much used in describing God, but this too has an indefiniteness that lacks the passion and poignancy which it possesses in our closest human relationships.

They lack that understanding of the kinship of God which was so marked in the adolescent Jesus. And that experience of the Galilean is to be considered the normal one toward which our religious training should tend. When adults are truly religious at home, intermediates develop that awareness of God and the eager responsiveness of soul which were displayed in the remarkable visit to the temple. But most parents and teachers have failed conspicuously. The religious attitude has not been caught by or developed within the majority of our adolescents. God has been thought of as a fact, but he has not become to them a living reality — a joy-giving and life-determining Comrade. We seldom know the extent of adolescent bewilderment about the character of God. And not knowing, we falter feebly in our attempts to explain current theology.

The case is not different with their knowledge of Jesus. In spite of years of attendance at the church school, young people go to college or to summer conferences with almost no idea of what Jesus was like when he walked among men. That he faced temptations like their own has never occurred to them. The " reproduceable experiences " of Jesus have been ignored or minimized.

He has become the strange wonder-worker of a past age rather than the guide and the approachable ideal for young and old of the twentieth century. The term which young people prefer in speaking of Jesus is " friend," and yet this expresses a wish rather than an accomplished understanding or experience. Though many would follow him, they do not recognize him when they see him, nor do they comprehend his teachings any better than did many of his obtuse admirers in the first century. " Love," again, is the word about which they have heard. And this is, indeed, an excellent point at which to begin our explanation and demonstration of the character of Jesus. That much is to the credit of the later generations of Christian teaching: love has been recaptured as the heart of the Master's gospel. But how vague and abstract it all is.

Religious education ought to reveal the universe more completely than science does. It must accept the analytical spirit and the honest methods of science, but it must also interpret the facts from the standpoint of religious faith. It must insist upon the reality of the non-material which gives significance to all things physical. It must declare with the conviction of a tested faith that there is a friendliness, a goodness in the universe, which is humanity's greatest possession.

2. To aid in facing the ethical and social problems of the immediate present and the far future. When young people hand in lists of the problems which perplex them, a single set of questions will probably show a juxtaposition of queries like the following: " How can we know what God is like? " " Should I, a girl of fifteen, go with one fellow or with a number of fellows? " " How can I decide wisely upon a life work? " Which question is important, which trivial? Shall we laugh at the silliness of youth in presenting the second query as a matter of vital concern? The fact is, there are scores of problems of this sort, having to do with relationships to the older generation, to the other sex, and to particular individuals and groups, and constituting the major social problems of adolescence.

Decisions now made in these "little" matters, standards accepted or rejected, attitudes and controls established, determine the weighty decisions of later life as well as the essential quality of life itself. The adult who laughs these off or frowns them down will find youthful hearts and lips closed against future confidences. The leader who dogmatizes or exhorts or scolds will produce equally disastrous results. These are natural middle-adolescent interests. The adult to whom they are revealed should be both proud and humble that his young people have opened their hearts to him, and should proceed patiently in helping them to see their way through the various possibilities.

Everything which presents difficulties to growing life is legitimately a part of the content of the church-school curriculum. There is no better place to discuss these matters than under the roof of the church, unless it be under the roof of a truly Christian home. Far too few young people share their confidences with parents. The church-school leader should be equipped and ready to serve in lieu of the parent if the opportunity presents itself. Subjects which are discussed with eager curiosity but little knowledge and under the lure of false ideals on street corners and in "bull sessions" had better be considered within the church. The necessary prerequisite is an adult leader, open-minded, intelligent, and loyal to Christian convictions. In the regular schedule of "lesson courses" and group activities, a definite place should be made for those ethical and social problems which represent the needs of youth. "Content courses" should be studied with present and future problems in mind. The leader should be ready to discard the scheduled program, if some specific issue bursts forth from the group with a spontaneity which reveals the pressing character of the problem. And it should not need to be said that what goes on in group sessions must be supplemented by personal comradeship, with its manifold opportunities for confidential conversations.

3. To create an intelligent and active loyalty to Christian ideals. It is not sufficient to talk about fundamental issues or to engage in purposeful enterprises. Even right thinking is not enough. If human life is to move upward toward the character of Jesus, we must grow a generation of young people who have convictions — convictions which are their own and for which they are willing to sacrifice and suffer. There must be a committal to the noblest of life purposes, and a frequent reconsecration to the leader whom we profess to follow. This will involve church membership, loyalty to the young people's organization. But much more fundamental is the necessity of understanding the demands of Jesus upon modern life, and of securing the unreserved allegiance of youth to the will of God. The ultimate objective of Christian education should be to develop Christians; Christians alive to their responsibility for making the purposes of God regnant in all the relationships of life.

4. To help young people gain the power to do what they know to be right. When our educational process has run its course, we still face the question, " But how can we be sure that these young people will do, will be able to do, those things in which they believe? " Discussion hours, in which high-minded young people have agreed of their own volition that certain actions are right and others are wrong, are immediately followed by conduct which belies their sincere intentions. Correlation of intellect and energy is lacking. Like Paul of old, " not what I would do, that do I practice; but what I hate, that I do." At this point, education must lean heavily upon religion.

The emotions are primary. Much of the wildness of youth is emotion in explosion. Religion, too, is as much a matter of the emotions as of the reason and muscles. Whether it be right to say that worship is the very essence of religion, that it is religion itself, it is safe to assert that the distinctively Christian attitude cannot be fully realized or maintained without worship. Only as we use the resources which come from communion with God are we able to develop the controls and to establish those habits which are consistent with our ideas of Christian morality.

5. To assist young people in becoming intelligent world-citizens. It is easy to confine interest within a very small circle. The middle adolescent is chiefly concerned about himself and his own group. It is a primary function of religious education to enlarge that circle until it includes all mankind. In addition to the inward look and the upward look there must be the outward look. Youth needs to learn to appreciate and to fulfill its obligations to the home, the older generation, children, the community, the nation, lands across the seas, the past, and the future. Study must be closely allied with practical enterprises of a social nature. Service activities must not be something added to the program; they form the basis for study, or grow out of study, or are parallel with study — all part of the comprehensive program for youth.

Here the adult leader needs both the inclination and the information to free himself from prejudices and smug opinions, in order that all the issues of life may be faced in a truly Christian spirit and on the basis of scientific knowledge. Adults must be in a continuous process of learning. We shall fail the new generation unless we approach the problems of social relationships in the spirit of the Christian student. To this must be added the courage and the self-abandon of the crusader.

6. To provide opportunities for sharing in significant service. In what has already been said, emphasis has been placed upon the necessity of service as an outcome of study, or as the basis of discussion, or as an accompaniment to the Sunday program. This is so vital, however, that it should be set down as a separate objective. It is important both because of its contribution to the character and training of youth and because there is so much that needs to be done.

It is a sadly contented church which has no overwhelming program planned for its membership, centered in definite objectives which arise from human need. High school young people think that they are busy, but when they are challenged by a worthwhile task, in which they assume some initiative and for which they bear responsibility, there will be a quick response. We have too often called upon them in behalf of causes regarding which they knew little and for which they consequently cared less. We have given them "flunky jobs" — important details, but not quite up to their felt dignity. These smaller duties they will undertake provided we have first depended upon them for larger tasks. It may seem an illogical procedure. It may appear unwise to trust them with big responsibilities until we have seen fidelity in small matters; it will be argued that the young should be content with subordinate places. But logic must retreat before human nature, before the disclosures of psychology. Young people, rightly or wrongly, have the opinion that their abilities are underestimated. The continual assignment to ticket-selling jobs and to the singing of songs at old folks' homes (important though this may be) reinforces this judgment.

Many of the most difficult undertakings upon which the church has embarked, or which it should attempt, could be brought to a successful conclusion if the interest and activity of the young were enlisted. Whereas middle age usually brings conservatism and a lack of daring, young people, when truly interested, are not troubled by tradition or a sense of the impossible. They venture where older people fear to tread and dare what has appeared both unreasonable and impossible, though desirable.

Leaders for the Future

We must always remember that we are preparing youth for both the present and the future. Our activities must have the wider perspective in mind. Many of our most important problems can be faced helpfully only as we relate them to the future. A case in point is the relationship between the sexes. During the present era of rebellion against the restrictions imposed by past codes, adolescent life is too much determined by its own limited knowledge and by its impulses. These teen-age youth will some day be heads of households, parents of children. Is it not essential that as we think of the immediate desires and temptations of adolescence we shall face them and solve them in terms of life in the large? The same is true of the relation of high school life to college experiences. Either through direct study or through indirection, it is important that such help be given to high school pupils as will serve them in good stead when they enter upon their college experience. The best way to solve the " college problem " is to keep it from arising by a wise solution of the " high school problem " — a high school problem which has its past and future as well as its present. So one of the primary objectives of all young people's work is that of producing an adulthood which shall be intelligent, open-minded, loyal to Christian conviction, and skilled in the art of living. All that has been said regarding the objectives for adolescent religious education has had in mind the development of the Christian adult as an ultimate result.

7. To train for future Christian leadership. The church seeks to leaven the whole lump. It aims at the development of a genuine religion among adults. But it is also interested in producing skilled leaders to undertake those responsibilities which are peculiarly its own. The training of young people for such leadership — both for the specialized forms of the Christian ministry and for voluntary lay service — is a significant phase of its program.

One of the finest fruits which has come from the traditional organizations for young people is the ease and readiness with which the graduates of classes and societies have assumed important rôles in the adult program of the church. This is convincing proof that one learns by doing; for classes and societies, to a very large extent, have given young people a chance to conduct their own programs. But leadership must be based upon information, too. In itself, doing is not sufficient training. It is important that able young people shall be introduced to specialized leadership courses within their regular curriculum, in community and church training schools, in summer conferences and camps, at district institutes and schools of methods.

It is not a case of " either-or." While pursuing special studies the young people need opportunities to try their skill. It is an utterly false position to aver that " we want to train these young people to lead so that they can take our places when we are done." The church which reserves all important duties for the years of middle or old age will discover that many of these potential leaders will have slipped away, having found other realms in which to use their abilities. The church, on the other hand, which assigns responsibilities to its younger members discovers that it is providing the soundest type of education for its youth, and is insuring its own future through the development of a large company of skilled leaders.

Secondary Objectives

Such objectives as those which have been discussed can be realized only through a process which includes study, service, worship, and comradeship. Certain additional suggestions may be noted as means by which the goals projected may be achieved. These means of reaching the main ends of adolescent religious education may well be thought of as secondary objectives, having great value in themselves.

1. Providing a wholesome social fellowship. The church and its departments no longer have so exclusive a field in the area of social fellowship as was the case two generations ago. The schools are increasingly directing the leisure-time activities of teen-age young people. Commercialized entertainments make it hard for the church to provide social events which can compete successfully for the interest of both old and young. Most churches do not need to offer so many social features as were necessary in other days. But the young people's organization will not thrive without some program of fun, nor can boys and girls be bound together into a genuine fellowship without frequent recreational features. Play is one of the essentials in any complete development of life. If young people are to grow into a fullness of Christian character, the church must give them the opportunity to play together as well as to study and pray and work together. A schedule of recreational events, planned and carried forward by groups of young people, will prove an effective means by which they will come to an experience of the joyfulness of the Christian life. It will help to knit them together into a fellowship, united in striving for the higher objectives to which the church of Christ should be devoted.

2. Furnishing an opportunity for coöperation with adults in the general program of the church. Every precaution must be taken to prevent the class, troop, department or society from becoming an end in itself. The same may be said of the church: it is a means to ends; it is an organized body of fallible persons with a loyalty higher and prior to that of the organization. The Christian church, despite trivialities and imperfections, remains the central agency through which the interests of Christ are mediated throughout the world. The personal institutional loyalty of young people as they grow into adulthood will be to the church —

not to troops, movements, departments. Once the duty of the church is clear, all its departments should move coöperatively in seeking to make and to carry forward an effective program.

One of the most serious possibilities of our meticulously departmentalized organization is that we are in danger of separating too closely into age-groups — intermediates being sufficient to themselves, seniors concentrating upon their own program independently arranged, adults going their way and giving little thought to the adolescent enterprise. Every wisely built program will provide that those things which can best be done alone shall be so accomplished. But the entire church needs the sense of solidarity and the power of achievement which come from fellowship in instruction, worship, recreation and service. Young people who participate in the joys and responsibilities which result from a genuine family life within the church will understand better the social implications contained in the gospel of Christ.

3. Coöperating with other Christian young people, in the community and throughout the world. No matter how interesting and successful the work of a local group may be, it misses something of inspiration, power and outreach if it has no affiliations beyond its own parish. Few churches have been satisfied to have no denominational attachments. Restricted vision and influence are almost certain to result from complete independence.

The areas of affiliation depend upon local conditions. They may be denominational, community-wide, or international and interdenominational. It is hoped that increasingly the state councils of religious education will become the agencies which are truly representative of all the forces of religious education, committed to purposes as prophetic as those of Jesus and to procedures consistent with the findings of scholarship. Once the component groups have thought out carefully the major objectives for Christian work among young people, it ought to be comparatively easy to agree upon certain elements of program which may be carried out coöperatively. Loyalty to interchurch agencies need in no way detract from the independence of the local unit. On the contrary, the wider fellowship will quicken the creative spirit. Complete Christian living cannot be achieved so long as so-called Christians are partitioned into noncoöperative groups.

Two general principles may be set down: (a) Whatever can be done as well coöperatively should be done together even though each unit may be required to make some sacrifice of program elements or leadership; (b) General objectives, and corresponding programs, may be constructed in large outline by the interchurch group, the details regarding methods, materials, objectives which are unique to a particular communion, and areas of activity being committed to the constituent church bodies. Young people are together in their school and community life. Artificial lines often keep them apart in religious activities. One of the significant contributions which this generation of youth can make is that of thinking and working together so that these lines of demarcation will grow imperceptibly faint. This is bound to come as they seek earnestly to realize the ultimate objective of religious education: that of building Christian character within individuals and of fashioning the social order according to the will of God.

Materials Recommended for Further Study

Athearn, Walter S. *Character Building in a Democracy.* Macmillan.
Bower, William C. *The Educational Task of the Church.* Bethany Press.
Coe, George A. *The Motives of Men.* Scribner's.
Coe, George A. *A Social Theory of Religious Education.* Scribner's.
Drake, Durant. *The New Morality.* Macmillan.
Emme, Earle E. and Stevick, Paul R. *Principles of Religious Education.* Macmillan.
Fiske, George W. *Purpose in Teaching Religion.* Abingdon Press.
Harper, William A. *Youth and Truth.* Century.

Howlett, Walter M., editor. *Religion the Dynamic of Education.* Harpers.

Religious Education (magazine), January 1928, February 1928, October 1928.

Shaver, Erwin L. *Present-Day Trends in Religious Education.* Pilgrim Press.

Soares, Theodore G. *Religious Education.* University of Chicago Press.

Weigle, Luther A. and others. *The Teaching Work of the Church.* Association Press.

Chapter II

THE ORGANIZATION OF YOUNG PEOPLE'S WORK

As in the determination of objectives so in the organization of forces, the local church must make its own decisions. This, too, is a matter for detailed study. The ideal or ultimate arrangement will be slow in arriving. Indeed, no organization can be considered final or fixed. Details must change to meet the successive needs of growing youth. The purpose of organization is to achieve results in personal character and in social life. The young people, therefore, must be organized in that way which will best realize the objectives agreed upon.

A new church, without traditions and institutional loyalties, will have a comparatively simple task in sketching the outline of its young people's organization. Its committee must work diligently, of course, but its final decision will not be hampered by outmoded structures which should be remodeled or razed. It will need to acquaint itself with the outstanding theories of organization; it should observe the experiences of typical churches which are using the various forms; it must consult the young people themselves, not after decisions have been reached but when the study is initiated. The resulting plan will probably meet with general approval, and immediate steps may be taken to realize it.

But most of our churches cannot start *de novo*. Their problem is more complicated. Although the committee may give hearty approval to a plan, it may be unable to adopt it at the time, in pure form, or in detail. Theories have to be studied in the light of actual situations; existing conditions cannot be ignored; leaders must not lose their constituencies or walk so fast that they discourage those who have been walking a long time though at a slower pace. Each plan of organization has its merits and defects; it must stand on its own feet. The enthusiastic support given it by a noted Doctor of Philosophy should not be regarded as sufficient evidence of its superiority. Nor does the fact that a certain plan worked well ten years ago, or that it is now flourishing in the other half-dozen churches of the community, prove that it is necessarily the best for this church. The convictions of the professor and the experience of the neighboring churches are to be taken into account along with other evidence.

A committee, large enough to represent the viewpoints of every existing agency, made up of old and young and including some who approach the whole matter free from attachments to existing or proposed agencies, ought to be appointed in a large number of our churches to study the question, "In order to realize our objectives for young people's work, what organizational framework is needed?" This is a project requiring more than two or three hours of discussion.

It may be of help to indicate some of the possible elements in the procedure. A draftsman, either professional or amateur, will be of great help. Perhaps a high school boy, interested in drawing and mathematics, may be found to serve. It would be a great joy to such an adolescent to be invited to assist. The charts which would help to visualize the situation include:

A demonstration of the correlation, lack of it, conflict or overlapping of existing organizations.

Age groups or types of adolescent life for which there is no functioning organization.

The number of young people served by each agency.

The number who belong to one, two, or three of the organizations.

The statistical success or failure of each agency during a five-year period.

The amount of time consumed by each agency during a week.

The amount of time needed if the best work is to be done.

The number of adult leaders required by each, and any resulting problems of leadership.

An outline of the various plans proposed.

The study would certainly take account of such questions as the following: Just exactly what is each agency attempting to accomplish? How successful is it? What are its failures and their causes? Are its achievements and shortcomings inherent in the institution? Is it possible for existing organizations, singly or in coöperation, to achieve the objectives which we have already set for ourselves? If so, what further coördination is needed? If not, what readjustments (dropping of organizations, adding new ones, changes in those existing) are necessary? What reasonable assurance is there that these proposals will increase efficiency? Will they secure the hearty support of young people and their leaders?

Individual assignments or duties allocated to subcommittees will probably include: the reading of standard books on the theory of organization (being sure to study opposing viewpoints); understanding the principles recommended by the educational leadership of the denomination; observation of the working of the several types of organization and correlation in other churches; constant touch with the present activities and opinions of the young people in the existing organizations.

Young people representing these agencies should, of course, be full-fledged members of the survey committee. It is not always certain that those selected will truly represent the majority opinion of the church's adolescent groups. Minority opinions in these agencies should always be sought; they may more sharply reveal the deficiencies and suggest improvements. The executive committees of the several organizations may be charged with a simultaneous study of some of the related problems, and recommendations may be asked from them by the general survey committee. Care should be taken to urge the young people to make an honest self-examination; otherwise, they may simply seek the opportunity for self-justification or for a criticism of their leaders. Indeed, the general committee will have to check itself occasionally or it will lose the scientific spirit of survey and will become an organized body of criticism or justification.

With the findings all in, a report may suggest two main goals: first, the complete plan to be worked toward and to be consummated within a period not too far in the future; second, a series of detailed suggestions regarding immediate steps.

There may still be differences of opinion regarding policies. Great care should be taken throughout the study to carry on the investigations and discussions in such a spirit that complete coöperation will be secured for any arrangement which commends itself to most of the leaders. It will be unfortunate if any major matters are settled by a close vote, by a mere majority. If such good-spirited unanimity is to be secured in the end, it will be only because the entire proceeding has been carried out in the spirit of free and earnest search, there being no effort to "put something over," to "kill" any organization, to make one agency the means by which all of the others must be correlated. Representatives of the organizations to be correlated must come into the study as equals. These precautions, which it would seem almost gratuitous to suggest, are here emphasized because organizational loyalty is amazingly strong. Many of our most serious conflicts center about institutional attachments. If the main objects of Christian work are kept to the forefront, it should be possible to reach unanimous conclusions and to secure complete coöperation, even though personal inclinations may be in other directions.

Guiding Principles

1. **The organization must be built so as to aid educational procedures.** Social clubs, " pep organizations," mass bodies are not to be taken as models. Work with young people must be along educational lines. This suggests a system like that of the public schools. We have had Sunday schools for more than a century but they have possessed few of the characteristics of our public schools. Modern religious educators have, therefore, been attempting to outline a system of religious education comparable to general education in method, materials, organization, and administration.

There is so little time provided for religious education. The Sunday-school class seldom has had more than half an hour a week for instruction, with that much more for worship, fellowship, and business. If the class could have the time now divided among several other organizations, a more effective piece of work might be done. This fact provides one of several arguments in favor of a single organization for each group of young people. If the group which meets on Sunday evening were the same organization which met in the morning, with the same leader, the program might naturally be an extension or an application of the points considered in the morning; the third session during the week would proceed along the same line. It is clear that if this worked out as proposed, there would be at least three hours of work each week by the young people of each class or department.

The realists argue, however, that it will not be possible to have this three-hour plan adopted in any considerable per cent of our churches. Their contention is that it is better not to tamper much with organizations but to concentrate upon content of program, and to secure as much unity in procedure as possible without disturbing existing agencies. It can be pointed out also that many of the best educational results in the day school come outside of formal processes, that clubs and similar agencies are often the best training forces of the school. So with separate organizations for the evening and weekday program. Their greatest accomplishments, it is said, are due to the fact that they are free and separate from the more formal processes of the Sunday school. It would also be unwise to ignore the fact that there is a mind-set among young people against the idea of making Sunday work like school work. This is not an insurmountable difficulty, but it is one of which many adult leaders are not aware.

The evidence on the comparative values of the two schemes is not very reliable. Certainly the old divided plan has been wasteful. There are not enough samples of successful unifications to lead to the conclusion that salvation lies in a single organization. We are still in the period of experimentation and probably shall be for a long time to come.

Whatever the decision of the local committee may be, two points should be safeguarded:

First, the program must be unified and comprehensive regardless of the number of organizations. This will involve some unity in organization, although it may not necessitate unification. There must at least be a council through which objectives and plans may be cleared. The council plan is practicable for ninety per cent of our churches.

Second, none of the young people's agencies should be unrelated to the educational program of the church. What goes on in any of them should contribute to the objectives agreed upon by the general committee. All methods which are uneducational should be discouraged; all program material which does not meet the educational standards should be discontinued; all activities should be planned in the light of the total scheme. Regardless of outside loyalties, the chief business of each of the agencies is to minister to the needs of these young people along lines agreed upon by the educational committee of the church. Great freedom to teachers and leaders should always be allowed, but this freedom must be exercised with reference to the fundamental aims of the approved educational scheme.

2. **Religious education is a voluntary enterprise.** This means that we must not draw too close a comparison with the public school system or organize our ideals and activities too strictly upon that basis. Adolescents are required by law, or by their parents, to attend school. Although the teaching and the courses may be boresome the pupils have to submit. Most young people do not have to attend Sunday school. The whole procedure in the church's program must be such as will appeal to youthful minds; otherwise, there will be no procedure at all, because there will be no young people.

This is the point at which many religious educational theorists become unreliable. They fail to take account of human realities. Here is a church where there has been a troop of Boy Scouts which included boys from Catholic families, under attractive leadership. The troop gave every superficial evidence of success. But the new director of religious education in a local church insisted upon important changes which were educationally sound — in the abstract. He maintained that the Scout program did not accomplish many of the specific aims for which the Protestant church stands; that these could not be introduced into the troop because of the presence of Catholics; that in order to achieve cumulative results the weekday activities should be under the leadership of the church-school teacher; the weekday program should be the class in action with reference to the primary interests of the instructional program; the Scout organization tended to develop a major loyalty to another body which seriously weakened the loyalty of the boys to the church school. Presumably the director may have been right in all points save two: he underestimated the abiding enthusiasm of the boys for their leader and he overestimated their opinion of the church school. The proposed changes did not work.

Here is the case of a pastor, back from an educational conference where the point was made that the programs in young people's societies are not educational and cannot be made so. The solution, he was confidently told, was to make the evening program a second session of the department which met in the morning, carrying the discussions of the school over into the evening meeting. His religious education committee approved the change. Unfortunately, there was no representative of the young people's society on the committee, or action might have been delayed or a general understanding secured. He announced his plan to the society; they remonstrated; he patiently explained the reasons for the change; they firmly insisted upon holding their own organization. The evening when the new plan was to go into operation a mere handful of young people attended the departmental meeting. Simultaneously, another group were holding their society meeting in a home, abetted by certain parents who held a sentimental allegiance to the national society. Matters grew worse. The pastor resigned. The society meetings, previously poor in content, grew worse rather than better. Actual unity of program was delayed by years.

The reverse situation is just as bad. A new pastor comes to a church. He finds that there is no young people's society, although the senior department flourishes with at least two sessions every week. He scoffs at the "high brow" schemes of religious educators, boasts of his loyalty to the Scout program and society work, and proceeds at once to undo the unified program which has been so carefully and fruitfully built up. His idea is to have at least three organizations where one was before; the more the merrier. "Young people," he says, "demand 'pep' in church life." But in this case the young people have been wholly satisfied while he alone demands "pep." Temporarily there is much furore and activity in the various organizations. But it flashes and dies. It is one more case of a dogmatic theory tenaciously held in spite of existing conditions wholly unfriendly to the theory.

3. **The departmental membership should be determined both by the age divisions recognized by psychologists, and by local social groupings.** Scholars agree that the years 12–14 (intermediate), 15–17 (senior), and 18–24 (young people) represent roughly the stages of adolescent development. It is clear that some fifteen-year-olds belong back with the intermediates and that some thirteen-year-olds deserve senior classification; but in our system, which must group according to approximate development, these divisions have usually been approved.

Where more than one organization exists an attempt should be made to correlate groupings and activities; that is, if the intermediate department of the Sunday school includes the 12 to 14 year olds, the intermediate society usually should be so graded. Thus, it will be possible for the programs to be supplementary, and many of the results desired by unificationists may be obtained by this method.

Numerous churches face the difficult problem of what combinations should be made where three departments are out of the question because of the small constituency. A large fraction of our churches must combine all young people within a single department — the equivalent of the young people's division, 12–24. In such a case it would probably be better to place the upper limit at 18 or 20. Equally good work cannot be done with such a wide diversity of ages; yet it must be admitted that some of our smaller churches, working under the least ideal conditions, are really doing the best work — just because they are putting the most into it.

As in other matters, the local leaders must decide what combinations are preferable. The following suggestions may help them to face the most serious complications. Intermediates and seniors are grouped together in thousands of churches. If it is at all possible to keep the intermediates in a single group, it should be done. Some intermediates will not be through the grade schools, and this fact alone will make them unwelcome to sophisticated seniors. The freshmen in high school and pupils in junior high school live in another world from that of the sixteen-year-olds. Even though they get along well together, the younger and older members do not think about the same problems or engage naturally in the same activities. Either the subject matter of class and society discussions will be in terms of senior interests and thus somewhat unintelligible to the younger members, or it will be along lines of intermediate interest and thus somewhat inane to the older young people. Only where conditions seem to make this a necessary combination or where special guarantees of success appear should these two groups be united.

The combination of seniors and young people also has its drawbacks, although the complications here are not so serious. There are two points of difficulty. The first is that high-school graduates have lost their interest in problems which center in school life, and much of the discussion of seniors inevitably pertains to school experiences. The second is that when young people are out of school they begin to live in an adult world, and their interests increasingly approach those of young married people and get farther away from teen-age experiences. If it does not seem possible to have separate groupings, the division line may be put at about twenty.

4. The plan should provide opportunity for both sex segregation and coöperation. The class divisions in the Sunday school have usually been on the basis of sex segregation. This is not a necessity so far as many of the courses are concerned, but it is, in general, a wise policy. Among intermediates and seniors many matters can better be considered when boys and girls are separated. With the growing frankness between the sexes there is a good deal to be said for combining the groups when they reach the older high-school years. At any rate, we dare not say dogmatically that the old plan must hold. If young people are reading and talking about the more intimate problems of life together at school and in automobiles, the church will do well to study the related issues with no false modesty, and in some cases, at least, it will be wholesome to do it in groups composed of both boys and girls.

Where class work is thought of in much larger terms than mere discussion, it is likely that the old plan of separation will be much more desirable, even in the older groupings. For the service activities and the fellowship features should tie the small group together in a closer unity than the larger mixed group will permit. The troop, for example, gets along much better than does a mixed class of boys and girls. Older boys like the secrecy and sense of "belonging" which their small organization affords, especially if they have a room of their own where they may meet during the week. Junior Brotherhoods and Young Women's Guilds, organized around classes or as classes, have a great appeal and usefulness.

But where this separation exists there must be specific activities which are carried out together. This is true even of intermediates where it may seem to be least needed. The Y.M.C.A. and Y.W.C.A. are recognizing the inadequacy of their programs in this regard, and are considering anew the means by which the coöperation of the sexes may be secured. The young people's societies have always understood the value of the combined plan and their history demonstrates that the young people like the arrangement. In the new plans of religious education the usual recommendation is that the classes be made up of a single sex, the departments to include the entire group. With this viewpoint we are in agreement, although it is well to suggest two reservations. The first is that the rule be not so fixed that any temporary shift will be difficult, for in any flexible program the time will doubtless come when certain issues can be better undertaken together. There should be no objection to combining classes for a quarter if conditions warrant. The second suggestion is that care be taken not to exalt the class so that it becomes the unit of all church work; the department should be a natural unit of as much importance as the class. Major activities should be undertaken by it. We shall but contribute to the already strong tendency to ignore the religious education activities after boys and girls are about fifteen years of age, unless they are joined in a large part of the religious program.

5. **The choice of a name is a project to be worked out by the local group.** This is true whether we think of classes, departments, or societies. It has been customary to call the departments by their technical designations: intermediate, senior, and young people's. If this practice is followed (and it is not necessary that it should be adhered to, for a significant name may be attached to a department as properly as to a club), the various classes should have distinctive names. While there are fond memories in some of our minds regarding the helpfulness of the leader of "Miss Carpenter's class," such designations are frequently unsatisfactory, both because Miss Carpenter may be teaching the class for a quarter only, and also because a helpful educational stimulus may be provided to the group which selects a name which will outlive the service of any particular teacher.

The recommended procedure is to appoint a special committee to study the matter of names, to invite written suggestions from members of the group, to make a list of names used in other churches, to secure recommendations from denominational and other religious headquarters, to propose from these the three or four which are most satisfactory to the entire group for final choice.

Certain widely used names should come into the consideration of the group. For example, many classes are identical with Scout troops and similar "activity agencies," and many more should become identical with them in churches where both exist. The Scout name may thus become the logical designation of the class. So, too, with classes affiliated with Y.M.C.A. or Y.W.C.A. programs; the Pioneer group within the church school will often be that class of boys which follows the Y.M.C.A. Pioneer program throughout the week. Some denominations have special names which they desire to have used in their local churches; they prefer that departments or classes shall adopt the name proposed by the central headquarters. With the growth of interdenominational coöperation through the Christian Quest program materials, there will be a tendency to organize classes or departments into Christian Quest groups. In thinking of the evening meetings, a primary consideration will be as to whether affiliation with a denominational or interdenominational fellowship is desired; that is to say, whether the group shall become an Epworth League, a Christian Endeavor Society, etc. The answer to this query should involve such questions as these: Can we do better work affiliated or unaffiliated? Do we need the wider fellowship in order to have the outreach that a local group covets? Will our program be broadened or narrowed by inclusion in such a national organization?

6. What should be the membership of the young people's organization? Membership in classes should be by definite assignment, just as enrolment in a given grade and appointment to a certain room at school is part of the administrative process. Where only one class for a given age range exists, new pupils will automatically go into that class; but where several classes of a given age exist, the superintendent of the department should make the assignment. Those who introduce new pupils to the school should take them to the superintendent first rather than try to predetermine the assignment by taking them to a particular class. In making his decision, the superintendent should not be arbitrary; the wishes of the pupil should be considered; inquiry should reveal the life interests and needs of the newcomer. In general, it should be true that young people should be placed among their friends or with those who share the same types of life experience. There are reasons why high school pupils and those who are earning their living should be put together in a single class. There are equally good reasons why they should be kept in separate groups. Certainly, where a different arrangement is possible, a new high school pupil should not be assigned to a class where the other members are non-students.

The membership of an age-group department is composed of all those who are in the classes for that particular age group.

The problems of membership are more complex when the evening groups are considered. Some of the possibilities are indicated below.

(a) Where complete unification prevails, the evening session is but the young people's department in a second meeting. There is here no question of membership, for all young people in the parish who are affiliated with the morning classes are members of the evening group, whether they attend or not.

(b) This same conception of membership prevails in many churches where the evening group is separately organized under a different name and with a separate set of officers. While this gives a desirable inclusiveness, it is doubtful whether a keen loyalty to the special objectives of the evening group is thus secured.

(c) Where separate organizations exist, the society group should work out its constitution carefully and in it should make specific provision as to how persons shall be admitted to membership. The simplest method is to vote in those recommended by the proper committee, without any formal commitment to a statement of principles.

(d) The customary method in Christian Endeavor and similar societies is to require allegiance to a pledge or a statement of purpose, this commitment usually being made in writing. In any group where serious work is to be done, new members should be faced with the obligations of membership and with the goals that are sought. The success of the Scout movement is due in no small part to the specific character of its requirements.

(e) Much of this pledging of allegiance to statements and causes is perfunctory and worse than meaningless. A study of the judgment of members of Christian Endeavor societies, for example, reveals a wide divergence of opinion regarding the usefulness of its "long pledge," by which members agree to pray and read the Bible every day, to attend all the Sunday and midweek services of the church, and to be faithful to a number of other details. One group insists that although members do not keep the pledge *in toto,* they have come nearer to living up to its ideals because they signed it than if they had not done so. Another group contends that the statement in the pledge, "unless prevented by some reason which I can conscientiously give to my Lord and Master," is the "most used part of the pledge." If this last statement is true, what is the moral effect of so easily signing so binding a requirement? Is it not an unethical practice to ask new members to agree to a course of action which the old members have not made a serious effort to follow out? There is, of course, objection to "toning down" the pledge to suit the desires of the crowd. But are the details of the "long pledge" of the Christian Endeavor society, and of similar local organizations, the most important matters? Would not more be accomplished by formulating a pledge which actually appeals to the best judgment of the local group, and which places the emphasis upon the "spirit" rather than upon the "letter"? Certainly it is inadvisable for local groups to accept ready-made a detailed pledge unless that is exactly the kind of statement which these particular young people want.

(f) A fundamental choice which every society or club must make if it approaches the membership problem seriously is whether it should be easier or harder to join the organization, whether the society should be an inclusive body or an eclectic group of those dedicated to the highest of spiritual goals. If the decision is in favor of the former ideal, the membership lists should be thrown open without much restriction — the policy of considering all young people of the parish as members will be a consistent one. If the society is thought of as a group of those who are striving to develop an intensive type of Christian life and activity, there should be a careful restriction of membership, and those invited to join should be impressed with the specific spiritual obligations upon which they are entering. Even so, an effort should be made to include as large a number as will meet the requirements.

7. The roster of officers should include such as are necessary to execute the program. Over-organization is as much to be avoided as under-organization. This point has already been emphasized with reference to a multiplicity of organizations; two agencies should not exist where one can do the work. Within a single group, care should be taken to provide for only those officers for whom there is a genuine function. Committee chairmen or members should not be appointed for ornamental purposes only, nor should a roster of officers be selected just because a "model constitution" makes provision for them. The usual functions of president, vice-president, secretary and treasurer will be required in almost every group. To these should sometimes be added such officers as adult counselors, representatives on the young people's council of the church, appointees to the official board of the church, delegates to the community interdenominational young people's council or union.

Most societies and some other agencies have more standing

committees than are needed. The theory is a good one that all members should be placed on committees, for this gives them a working loyalty to the organization. But in cases where there seems to be no real task for the committee there will be a bad ethical result: the committee does nothing, the new committeeman comes to underrate the responsibilities of officers, and the expected loyalty does not materialize. It is better not to appoint committees than to name members to bodies which exist largely on paper and for which there is no clear-cut function.

Most organizations will need four or five permanent committees, selected from such a list as the following: membership, program, finance, social, missionary, social service. The chairmen of these committees, together with the officers, constitute the executive committee, which is responsible for initiating and recommending most important items of business. In a class where the membership is small, there will be fewer committees — the officers serving as an executive committee, and special groups of two or three being appointed for specific tasks.

Permanent committees should hold stated meetings (usually monthly) with businesslike procedure, and should make regular reports to the executive committee and through it to the general body. One of the most needed elements in most of our young people's organizations is businesslike procedure. This is important not only for the sake of efficiency, but for the character development of youth.

The important consideration in deciding what committees shall be appointed is, What are the tasks to be undertaken? Those which are continuous and fundamental may require standing committees which should function throughout the year. Many other enterprises are seasonal or temporary. It is wiser to appoint special committees to carry out these projects — instructions being given as to the character of the responsibility, the time-limit, and the resources available. It is frequently found that persons charged with a specific duty, to be accomplished within a given period, will work with an intensive fervor which will produce far greater results than if the task were simply included within the series of responsibilities given to a standing committee. It is a common experience that many "standing" committees do little else than "stand."

Materials Recommended for Further Study

Cope, Henry F. *Organizing the Church School.* Doubleday, Doran.

Harper, William A. *An Integrated Program of Religious Education.* Macmillan.

Harris, Hugh H. *Organization and Administration of the Intermediate Department.* Cokesbury Press.

Maus, Cynthia P. *Youth Organized for Religious Education.* Bethany Press.

Mayer, Herbert C. *The Church's Program for Young People.* Century.

Stout, John E. *Organization and Administration of Religious Education.* Abingdon Press.

Thompson, James V. *Handbook for Workers with Young People.* Abingdon Press.

How a Leader Uses Organization. The International Council of Religious Education. (Christian Quest booklet.)

Scouting. The Boy Scouts of America.

The Commission Plan. American Baptist Publication Society. (Five booklets.)

The Standard Church Troop. The Boy Scouts of America.

Chapter III

THE CLASS CURRICULUM

THE curriculum has commonly been thought of as "something studied in the Sunday school," the collection of courses or materials to be covered by teachers and pupils during a certain period of time. Where there is a consistently planned effort to achieve such aims as those listed in the first chapter there is a curriculum or program worthy of the name.

The terms "program" and "curriculum" may well be used interchangeably. The former is the more practical word, understood by young people and adults alike. When it is used, it should refer to the whole range of activities in which the young people engage; that is to say, the "young people's program" includes all that goes on in all of the young people's agencies. The program of a given class includes weekday activities as well as the Sunday morning session. The word "curriculum" is a pedagogical term more commonly used by specialists; it, too, must be understood to include the total activities of the entire young people's division. There are no such things as "extra-curricular activities" — what goes on at socials, in Scout troops, in missionary projects is as truly a part of the curriculum as the discussion in the Sunday morning session. The curriculum may be defined as the program by which the organized forces of youth, with the advice of responsible adults, seek to accomplish desired aims.

Some Underlying Ideas

The programs projected by churches and religious education agencies rest upon a number of basic conceptions, five of which should be passed in review.

1. The four-fold emphasis. Educational theory has made a great deal of the four-fold life idea, and comprehensive programs of national organizations have been built upon it. Basic to this conception is the recognition of growing life as a process of learning, of communion with God, of human fellowship, and of energetic and purposeful activity. The programs constructed have centered around four types of group endeavor: physical, intellectual, social or service, and spiritual. The dominating idea is that of completeness, of the necessity of developing the whole personality, of engaging in a program which ministers to all human needs and interests. The church owes a great deal to those who initiated and promoted the four-fold emphasis.

But there is something artificial and partial in this idea. Life cannot be quartered. When we build the physical we are also involving the intellectual. One does not put an end to instruction, to the mental process, when he begins to worship or serve. It is quite possible, and somewhat helpful, to list a dozen activities and to label them "service," "recreation," "worship" or "instruction," according to the dominant characteristic — if that can be discovered. But to do this is to think of a program in terms of bits — bits which have worth but which do not represent any enterprise actually carried to a conclusion. It is time to think in terms of life as it is: a unit, consisting of experiences involving emotions, ideas, ideals, attitudes, principles, impulses, motives, actions. Our program should deal with important issues and activities, not because they fall within a category of "instruction" or "service," but because these issues and activities need attention.

2. The life situation approach. For many years, actual occurrences in personal or group life have been used as illustrations in Sunday school and society materials. The "life situation" is a form of the illustration. Broadly speaking, it may be an actual occurrence among the young people in the class or society, an event which has happened among other young people, an incident gleaned from fiction or history or biography, a "case" which represents either a normal or an abnormal situation, a hypothetical set of circumstances. In its use, it is essential that all details be made available, so that the study of the problem will be in the light of the conditioning or related circumstances.

The life situation may be used either as an illustrative element in the study of some selected question or theme, or as the whole basis of discussion. The group attempts to place itself in the circumstances in which the person involved found himself. By considering all the factors, it attempts to agree upon the right solution. Having done this the study may be concluded, it being deemed sufficient to have drawn the attention of the members to the case, and it being believed that they will face similar situations constructively because of their common study. Or, the answer to the particular situation may be used as the basis for the drawing up and discussion of general principles related to the larger theme.

For example, the group may proceed to discuss just a single situation, such as this: Elizabeth is one of five children; the parents are not "well to do"; the two older brothers and the one older sister have gone to work after finishing high school; Elizabeth's teacher urges her to go to college because she possesses unusual literary ability; she herself wants to go and has urged her parents to permit it, offering to earn a large part of her way through school; the parents say that they cannot afford it and that it would be unfair to the other children who did not have this opportunity; one of the older brothers sides with Elizabeth, the other two older children say little but seem to disapprove. What is Elizabeth's duty? One method of procedure would be simply to discuss the tangled factors in the case, and to try to discover what Elizabeth's duty is. Another method would be to use this life situation along with additional discussion material in an attempt to formulate answers to the problem: to what extent should young people do what their parents want? The advantages of the life situation method are that it begins with the concrete, it arouses interest at once, it points the way to emergencies which will sometimes need to be faced, and it may lead the young people to commit themselves to wise life principles.

The possibility is always present, of course, that it will not lead to wise conclusions, that there will be an inadequate consideration of the most important issues, and that there will be very little of positive character determination — that it will all end in talk, and that this talk may not be rewarding or intelligent. Except where the situation discussed is an actual local one, about which something must be done, the danger is that discussion will end the matter. There are, consequently, those who question the wisdom of using any life situation except that which is directly the present life situation of the group considering it. But this is to rule out of the program a vast amount of experience which young people need to draw upon, and to approve the policy of solving problems when you come to them rather than building a curriculum which will save young people from experiencing certain situations. It is a short-sighted policy which faces emergencies only when they arise; part of our task is to save the world from many unnecessary and character-ruining crises. It is important that a competent committee should select its problems carefully; otherwise, the curriculum will be partial and lopsided in the elements included as well as in the treatment given. The life situation approach is essential to any adequate program, but it must be combined with other ideas still to be considered.

3. The areas of human experience. A plan, used to a large degree by the Committee on International Curriculum of the International Council of Religious Education, is that which divides human experience into certain segments. After a careful analysis, it has been found that life relationships consist of the following main areas: health, education, economic, vocational, citizenship, recreation, sex and parenthood and family life, general life in the group, friendship, esthetic, specialized religious activities. Each of these has a vast number of ramifications. It is clear that if the curriculum is to be effective it must take account specifically of the situations within these areas and must enable young people to establish these various relationships in a Christian fashion. One of the simplest procedures would be to build a series of lesson courses around these eleven subjects. But in the construction of such a program, several other basic ideas would need to be taken into account, as will be indicated later.

By a proper combination with the elements contained in the two approaches already discussed and in those which follow in the next two sections, this approach seems to offer much hope.

4. Character traits as goals. In many of our most modern programs of religious education the emphasis is in the direction of inquiry rather than of crusade, of coming to conclusions regarding concrete situations without giving allegiance to basic standards of belief or conduct, of working out one's own judgments rather than accepting traditional principles or codes or ideals. This process, we maintain, should lead to strong convictions because they have been arrived at through diligent study and experience. It may, however, be a very wasteful process if it leads to a continuous reproving of things which have been eternally true and which need no further demonstration by the trial and error method. Goodness and purity and honesty are possessions of the race which should not be doubted; they do not need to be discovered anew by each generation through the experiencing of their opposites. Intemperance and sensuality and shiftlessness are traits from which we need to try to save our young people. If the method of facing life situations and of solving aright the problems within any area of human experience is to be fruitful, it is necessary that the leader shall have certain convictions, ideals and purposes. These he is not to try to enforce upon the young people with dogmatic fervor. At the same time, the function of a leader is to lead, to demonstrate. "Honest inquiry" and "individual and group creativity" are not enough. The leader is interested in a certain type of character. If the ambition for this type is lacking among the young, if ideals and high purpose are not prominent, the leader cannot rest content with the thought that some day they will stumble upon these ideals themselves.

The Committee on International Curriculum has, therefore, very wisely studied to discover what kinds of virtues or ideals or character traits the Christian church should be interested in developing. It has gathered a large number of positive and negative manifestations under twenty-two general heads and has included in its tentative plans for program-building the intention of trying to develop these positive elements of character: co-operation, courage, creativeness, dependability, faith, forgiveness, goodwill, health-mindedness, honesty, humility, joyousness, love, loyalty, obedience, open-mindedness, penitence, purity, purposefulness, reverence, self-control, self-respect, and spirituality.

5. The project principle. One of the most popular emphases today is that the program shall not consist of unrelated bits but of units, each of which is undertaken with a deliberate purpose and is carried to certain conclusions which involve all the energies of the group — ideational, emotional, physical. This means that for a given period the young people would be at work upon a certain task, a quest of discovery, a piece of service, the establishment of a certain type of relationship. Everything that is done by the group during this period makes some direct contribution to the major enterprise. It is expected not only that the results will be informational, but that positive personal and social fruitage will result — something will be done. The project involves the total group life together. This is an application of the doctrine that we learn by doing, and that we have not learned until we have put into practice that which we have been told, or we have posited or discovered. Such a curriculum, therefore, would be a series of enterprises to be expressed in functional terms rather than in bookish titles.

If there is a local leadership which will give the time and direction that it demands, this type of program should secure from the young people greater interest and more lasting results. It is foolish to say that young people cannot learn by the old method of exhortation, that we are merely wasting time by conducting discussions, that our manifold and unrelated service undertakings are in vain. But it is correct to say that these methods are inefficient in that they do not secure for us all the values that should be gained from the plan of coördinated enterprise. At the same time, we should not deceive ourselves into believing that the project approach will solve all our problems, that a person necessarily learns the truth and acts it and makes the desired "carry-over" into every personal and social situation just because in the church school he has gone through a program built on the project basis. It has not yet been demonstrated that because a group has carried on a project in friendliness with children in Mexico it will form those permanent attitudes of good will which are needed toward the Italians within their own neighborhood. Nor is it certainly true that because they have conducted a project in good will among the Negroes across the tracks they will also develop sympathetic and fair-minded attitudes toward the people of Russia. Too much is claimed for the project idea, just as too much is claimed for each of the other educational theories. But in all of our curriculum-building and in all of our teaching we must give a larger place to this unified approach, to the combined use of all human resources in the accomplishment of the chosen task.

Types of Class Courses

Generally speaking the programs in our classes center around the Sunday morning "lesson hour," if, indeed, this is not the whole of the program. Theoretically, this small group is supposed to be the unit for a complete series of rounded activities — service, social, and worship as well as study and discussion. These other elements (the primarily non-instructional ones) continue, however, to be carried on largely by the more inclusive groups — department and society — and it is not our purpose to insist that the class shall be the central unit for the adolescent program. The department seems much better suited to conduct most of the worship, to carry on a considerable portion of the social activity, and to undertake many of the service activities. At the same time any adequate studying of a "course" will provide some outlet for the expression in action of the good impulses and worthy ambitions; it is equally true that the best way of approaching many problems is through the physical activity undertaken by the class as a unit; the project idea in teaching requires some such combination. While we do not agree that printed courses or outlines of Sunday discussions constitute the central or most important element in the curriculum, we face the fact that most classes do have some kind of course, some kind of "lesson period." It is still true that for a majority of these groups, the content of the class session is the point of departure for whatever unified program there may be.

1. The uniform lessons. There are still too many schools which use these materials, a single piece of Scripture being the basis for the teaching in all the classes on a given Sunday. The plan emphasizes "knowing the Bible." Certain definite portions of the Bible are used as the foundation for general class discussion. Lesson writers seek to find some modern application for each age group, but those who have had experience in writing the materials know how difficult it is to find such applications for many portions of the Scripture, especially for the younger pupils. Those who have tried to lead a class know, also, how hard it is to make the point of contact between modern youth and certain of the abstract or historical sections of the Bible. The uniform lessons should be reserved for that part of adulthood which is interested in the interpretation of Bible passages; they have comparatively little usefulness for adolescents. Not that many of us have not profited by the wise use which teachers made of them while we were young, but it is unethical to continue to use them when they are woefully inadequate and when there are other types of materials much better suited to youthful needs. They make, under the best leadership, only a feeble contribution toward the accomplishment of aims like those enumerated in the first chapter.

2. Graded lessons. It was to meet the need of specialized emphases at different age levels that the graded lessons were prepared. Both the closely graded and the group graded rest upon the conviction that certain interests are prominent during the intermediate age, others during the senior. It is the business of religious education to recognize these interests and to provide help specifically adapted to these emergent requirements. This is psychologically and pedagogically sound procedure. No school can carry on a program sufficient for the needs of life unless it recognizes the fundamental necessity of grading its work.

The graded lessons present problems as well as resources.

First, the judgment of the graded lesson committees must not be considered final and infallible. Their work represents the fruit of diligent investigation. They have done for all of us what none of us could do adequately for ourselves. Yet few of the scholars would insist that they have arrived at ultimate conclusions. They have discovered interests and needs which seem to be widespread at a given age. They have suggested teaching points and emphases which will usually contain help. But some twelve-year-olds require fifteen-year-old treatment and *vice versa*. The special needs of a "gold coast settlement" and of a Hull House settlement must not be subjected to exactly the same treatment. There must be specialization upon other bases than age gradation. The local committee should seldom accept the entire graded series. It is only occasionally that any single series seems to meet all conditions satisfactorily. Careful specialization along such lines as the following is needed: school or industrial interests, home backgrounds, racial conditioning, economic situations, cultural development, mental diversity, etc.

Second, the materials issued are unequal in value. This criticism applies in two directions. In the first place a number of publishers take the general outline of the lessons prepared by the interdenominational committee, secure their own writers, and give their publications such names as "Pilgrim Graded Series," "Constructive Studies." There are available, therefore, to the local school several series of International Graded Lessons, based upon the same general plan but varying greatly in their theological viewpoints, their ethical and social outlook, their use of educational method, and their adaptability to the so-called average school. Local committees should not accept any particular set without comparing the merits of similar publications from other presses.

Even within a single series, such as the Pilgrim Series, there is wide variety. A class may be delighted with the practical character of this year's textbook. It may look forward to next year's work with eagerness, expecting that the method and material will be as useful as that of the year just closed. But it discovers that another author has prepared this particular text. His viewpoint is entirely different. It may be academic whereas last year's approach was highly practical. It was a great advance when schools substituted a complete series of graded lessons for the uniform, but we must go beyond that. If the general outline of the graded lessons is accepted, the local committee should study each year's work in the light of the offerings of the several publishers. This may mean that Course VIII will be a Pilgrim publication, Course IX a Scribner booklet, Course X a University of Chicago Press outline.

Third, most of the graded lessons are still constructed largely in terms of a one-period study or discussion. The Presbyterians are working on a program by which the entire activities of an age group will be correlated. The new Closely Graded Church School Courses for the intermediate department are built on a two-session basis, which may be used either on Sunday morning and a week day, or on Sunday morning and evening. But it still remains for the local leaders to adapt the materials within most courses so that the range of activities will be more far-reaching than an hour's study or discussion.

3. Elective courses. Increasingly the most progressive schools, both large and small, are building their class curricula on an eclectic basis. They recognize thereby that a program must be truly a local program. The responsible committee, therefore, considers graded lessons along with others, but it feels under no obligation to be partial to them. It begins with the young people in the particular church. If the graded series has elements which correspond to the felt needs, some of these courses will probably be incorporated into the local plan, but there is no predisposition in favor of the subjects or materials offered by denominational or interdenominational curriculum-makers. Of course, any sensible local leader will be humble enough to know that the men who have been giving years to a study of the problems of the curriculum have information which he does not have, and will agree that it would be folly to ignore the results of their study. In certain areas, too, in which his particular denomination has a distinctive mission or interest, he will rely greatly upon the suggestions which come from the responsible national leaders.

First, there is the "lesson course" which is essentially "content-centered." There has been a justifiable revolt against this type of material. For a long time most of our quarterlies and texts were of this character. They contained a certain amount of information to be passed on by teacher to pupil, or to be absorbed in home reading and class discussion. The idea was to furnish information. It is too much to say that this was the only idea, for probably no course has ever been written which did not have behind it also the intention of molding the personal life of the pupils. It was supposed, however, that the gaining of information was the primary means by which this result might be accomplished. We do not want to go to the extreme of saying that information is not a valuable and necessary element in the procedure, or that the impartation or discovery of a factual content is not worth the time that a class may spend on the process. It is correct, however, to say that a class or school which builds its whole curriculum on the theory that the impartation of information is the essential or primary purpose is short-sighted and inefficient.

There are certain courses which may well continue to be "content-centered." Young people want or need to know facts about the history of the church, the origin of the Bible, the progress of the Christian enterprise abroad, the respective spheres of science and religion. To read good books on these subjects is one of the best means of securing information. To engage in serious study of available materials is a worthy function of the church-school class. There is a good deal of slighting comment about "content-centered courses" today which overlooks the perennial need of hard and deep study on the part of our young people. Some of our newer methods which make the class hour interesting and lively do not compel hard thinking based upon hard study. Upon many of the fundamental issues of growing life the only possible way by which sufficient information can be gained to justify what may rightfully be called personal conviction is through the reading and discussion of sound and solid books which are largely "content material." But even with reference to such subjects as those just mentioned, it will be necessary to do more than read, or listen, and think.

Second, there are those which may be called content-discussional courses. A common outline for such a course is to begin with certain factual considerations, laid out in considerable detail in the text. Closely related to these facts is a series of discussion problems based on life-situations and thought-provokers. Such a procedure recognizes the need of providing adequate information for discussion or activity. If, for example, the course is an attempt to interpret the life and teachings of Jesus to a modern generation, the Bible text will be the first material to be studied. There will also be certain interpretative paragraphs which give something of the setting out of which the teaching arose. This will be followed by several "cases" out of modern life, which present problems similar to those which Jesus faced. The discussion will very likely be lively regarding the issues involved in these modern situations. The final purpose will be to assist the young people to make their decisions regarding these present-day cases in the light of the Biblical record of Jesus' experience and teaching.

Third, there is the topical-discussional course. This is similar to the content-discussional type, but the process is reversed. Instead of beginning with the study of a certain amount of Biblical or literary material and then attempting to relate it to present-day living, the starting-point is a very specific modern issue. As source material intended to help the young people to answer the question which is the subject for study, both Biblical and non-Biblical materials are provided.

Fourth, there is the course which follows the project idea. It will probably not begin with content material or a discussion question, but with an enterprise to be undertaken. If it is to be truly a local undertaking, it is difficult to see how any printed material can give much more than a statement of method and a suggestion of source material. This project may be a very specific one, such as establishing right relationships with the people of other races in the community; or it may be a more general one, such as attempting to come to right conclusions regarding the attitudes which Christian young people should have to the people of other races. Each of these would probably involve many of the same elements. A project may begin with an activity of service and may then involve study and discussion as part of the program, or it may begin with study and discussion and then involve service as an outcome or as a step in the program. The important thing is not where one begins, but how much is involved in the process and where the program leads.

Not every course needs to be a project course. There is such a thing as worship for the sake of the experience one gets out of it. There is such a thing as reading and studying for the joy and general good that result, a value which cannot always be estimated at the time and whose outcomes cannot be measured, either immediately or in the future, by any available tests. The church-school program cannot be evaluated simply by immediate pragmatic tests. Education and religion are not to be subjected at every point to utilitarian investigations. But for two reasons the curriculum must include the project idea. The first is that we have so little time to accomplish the aims in which we are interested that we must bring to completion any process in which we are engaged unless we want to waste both our time and the lives of our youth. The second is that young people are desirous of giving time to those enterprises which seem to issue in convincing conclusions — conclusions which are not simply intellectual but which make a difference in social life.

Fifth, there is that class procedure which has neither a con-

sistent method nor a continuous program. It may seem to some to be a hit-or-miss affair. Whether it is that or the most effective scheme of all depends almost entirely upon the leader. In not a few schools some of the best work is being done by a leader who has no set course, no textbook and no fixed plans. He meets with a group of boys each week and discusses matters which are "hot points" at the time, relating the activity of the week to the same interests. Sometimes a single subject involves the discussions and activities of several weeks. Sometimes a single hour disposes of the problem. Sometimes discussion ends the matter; on other occasions investigation and service grow out of the class session. The close contacts between the members of such a group result in confidences and intimate pursuits wholly impossible to those classes which proceed more formally.

But there is danger in this lack of plan. The leader must make more careful preparation than if he had a fixed course. He must be certain that the morning hour is not wasted in irrelevant talk. He must constantly be asking himself whether these young people are being introduced to information and experiences which develop character or are just passing the hours of the week in interesting club fashion. He must be sure that to those issues in which they have a present interest are added certain issues regarding which they need to develop an intelligent and Christian attitude. For it continues to be true in religious as in general education that one of the chief functions of the school is to prepare young people adequately to meet issues for which at present they have no concern.

How Shall We Build This Curriculum?

In the light of the various considerations introduced in this chapter, how shall the local leaders go about the business of determining the curriculum for the church-school classes? The following definite suggestions are recommended:

There should be a committee charged with the task of building the curriculum.

It should discover what the interests of young people are — both those which seem to be abiding and those only immediately insistent.

It should discover what the needs of youth are.

Having before it a list of these outstanding interests and needs, and having always as a background the major objectives which have been agreed upon for the religious education program, the committee should outline a tentative curriculum covering the several age groupings.

The committee will not consider its job done once for all.

Suggested courses, materials, or methods may also be indicated for the particular units. While this committee is charged with the duty of indicating texts, the teacher should not be held too rigidly to the decision of the committee. On the one hand, if the teacher wants to use something which is clearly not satisfactory, the committee should be firm; but frequently, the teacher is able to build his own outline, using a variety of materials and plans, and this is greatly to be desired.

The curriculum should not be confined to a strict quarter system, if another plan seems preferable.

Such adjustments should be made in the teaching force as will produce the best results.

There should always be a readiness to postpone a predetermined program if something suddenly comes upon the horizon which constitutes a "hot spot."

It should always be borne in mind that when subjects have been selected and materials provided, a curriculum has not been created. The curriculum or program is the ongoing activity. It includes worship and service and recreation as well as instruction. Therefore, the outline of the program must be such as to lead both teacher and pupil always to think in functional terms, terms which certainly lead to social effort.

Materials Recommended for Further Study

Betts, George H. *The Curriculum of Religious Education.* Abingdon Press.

Bower, William C. *The Curriculum of Religious Education.* Scribner's.

Charters, Werrett W. *The Teaching of Ideals.* Macmillan.

Dobbins, Gaines S. *Working with Intermediates.* Sunday School Board of the Southern Baptist Convention.

Finn, Elizabeth M. *Church Work with Intermediates.* Judson Press.

Maus, Cynthia P. *Youth and the Church.* Standard Press.

McKibben, Frank M. *Intermediate Method in the Church School.* Abingdon Press.

Shaver, Erwin L. *A Project Curriculum for Young People.* University of Chicago Press.

The Development of a Curriculum of Religious Education. Research Service Bulletin No. 5. The International Council of Religious Education.

Life Experiences and the New Curriculum. Research Service Bulletin No. 6. The International Council of Religious Education.

Program Suggestions for Group Leaders. International Council of Religious Education. (Christian Quest booklet.)

Religious Education (magazine), December 1926.

Chapter IV

THE PROGRAM OF THE YOUNG PEOPLE'S SOCIETY

THE young people's society movement spread rapidly because it met a neglected need: the need of an organization which the young people control themselves (but usually with the guidance or counsel of the pastor or an adult). It provides an opportunity for the expression of religious ideas, feelings and energies which many class programs in the past have not offered. Like most institutions, it eventually suffered a slump both in numbers and in influence. A primary reason for this decline is that the programs which local groups followed were made in wholesale fashion by professional program architects. This was in direct opposition to the genius of the original society. The chief characteristic of the society type of organization is that it draws out the potentialities of the young people in a plan of work which is distinctively their own. Of course, every group needs some help from the outside, and as the means for providing this help was strengthened, the policy came gradually and almost inevitably to be changed. The national offices became program-makers instead of program assistants; the function of the local committees changed from that of creators to that of acceptors. A nationally stereotyped scheme of organization and procedure spread throughout the land; local creativity and originality became the exception rather than the rule, and the society movement was on a retrogressive march.

At least three developments, characteristic of this third decade of the century, should be noted, for they are fundamental to any helpful consideration of program building:

1. There is greater autonomy in the society. Father Clark's original Christian Endeavor society was a little group of young people, with an adult, working out their program. This was the prototype for any successful similar organization. That is the way programs must be built today. That is the way they are coming again to be built. Autonomy in local programs with fellowship in common enterprises is the combination which furnishes the key to success.

But there is greater independence than this. A surprisingly large per cent of the young people's societies are organized independently of their national or interdenominational bodies. " Canned " programs from headquarters have proved unpalatable. Consequently, in considering a better diet, the local groups have ignored the recognized source of supply entirely. When a society died, there was little disposition to reorganize under the old name. Something new was adopted. There is something tragic in this, the tragedy resting in the fact that there is such great possibility in these interdenominational and international societies. They fit in with the psychology of youth: emphasis upon the broader fellowships, mass attack upon great issues. It is one of those crucial challenges to the world leadership of denominations and society organizations: are they big enough to allow the Christian young people of today to make of these organizations whatever they believe modern Christianity demands?

There is a decided weakness which comes from separation and independence. A mass of local units, each functioning by itself within a parish, lacks the power which the world needs and which youth should contribute. It is doubtful whether what has been lost can soon be regained, but certainly the honest efforts of national leaders should be in the direction of common objectives which might be offered to this conglomeration of independent groups. Actual unity in organization will be difficult to achieve. Identity of local programs, in details of content or method, must not be attempted; much of the surrendered territory has been lost because of this mistake; but great goals, fellowship in action among the groups organized under a variety of names, should unite our Christian young people in common endeavor. We must not only tolerate, but actively promote, the idea that the local society shall build a program which is uniquely its own. But out of this independence there must also come some united thinking and effort. Otherwise the growing generation of Christians will be less world-minded than the adulthood of today.

2. The teen age group has become increasingly important. A generation ago there were many teen age members of the young people's or intermediate societies. The control of the older society was usually in the hands of those in the early twenties, and the intermediate society was pretty much a preparatory group which really was not expected to function very creatively. It is still true that one of the banes of many a high school "crowd" is that the society is thought of by some well-intentioned people who are "seventy years young" as the possession of all who want to come. The local leadership should make it clear, in a kind but positive way, that the older people do not belong in the young people's society.

In the educational world, high-school young people are assuming much greater leadership than has ever been the case in America. There is more alertness and idealism among the high-school and college groups than among any other class of the American population; there is also unbounded energy and almost unlimited ability. The church loses its greatest asset, viewed from the point of numbers and of the stretch of years, unless its program at the high-school age be unusually interesting and significant. Both because of this new-found power and sense of status which has come to these seniors and because so many of our graduates now go away to college, the tendency has been to make the high-school group the bulwark of the young people's society movement.

It is easy to see what effect this lowering of the age level has had, or must have, upon the programs of the organizations. Discussion subjects must be modified. Service enterprises must be of such a nature as will be considered worthy of this group of self-important and able adolescents. The entire series of activities must help these young people to prepare for the experiences either of college or of vocation. The emphasis must be a middle adolescent one, instead of an older-young people's or younger-adult one. In many churches several societies will exist. The high-school organizations (or the intermediate and senior groupings) must not be considered merely as feeders for the older group. They must be thought of as equally important if not more important. Then, too, there is that specialized group of young people in college or university situations. The stereotyped society program can seldom be recommended for them.

3. Educational theory has advocated making the evening meeting a second session of the church-school class or department. The argument has been that it is unwise to have several organizations, made up of practically the same people. This argument has been particularly cogent in view of the fact that every class and department needs more time in which to accomplish the program expected of it. In addition, it must be said that the programs of societies have often been contrary to educational procedure; they have frequently counteracted or conflicted with the standards set for the church school; they have not been amenable to educational control through the responsible committee of the church.

It is not a matter of primary significance whether the evening meeting is conducted as a separate organization or as a phase of a single body's program. Most churches, however, need the benefits which the evening session can provide. It should, therefore, not be done away with unless its distinct function is taken care of in some other way at some other time. Whether this session is conducted as a phase of the department or class or as a separate program, it should be so developed as to make a connection with the morning and weekday activities. It is not right to insist that everything shall be correlated with the morning program. It is just as legitimate to reverse the process, although usually it will be found that the morning curriculum offers a more unified basis for correlation. A better way of looking at the whole enterprise is to think of the youth of the parish as a whole, of the variety of activities which need to be carried on by them and with them, and then to divide the responsibility among the several agencies or between the various sessions of the single body. The important thing is that one shall supplement the other, and that the two together shall make an appreciable contribution to the religious life of the young people of the community.

In this chapter, when the word "society" is mentioned, the reference is to any of these evening groups, whether a club, a league, a society, or a separate phase of the class or departmental organization.

Types of Local Situations

The conceptions of the evening meeting differ with denominations, with types of organizations, with local history, and with the educational theory of the adult leader.

1. The evening meeting as a second session of the class. Some of the new graded materials for intermediates are being built on a two-session basis, and the stories and discussion points offered for the second hour may well be carried over to the Sunday evening session instead of being reserved for the weekday meeting. In a few cases, materials have been prepared on a similar basis for seniors. The difficulty, to date, has been that the ideas presented for the second session have had little appeal. They have been a series of uninteresting questions based upon the contents of the morning lesson, questions which were doubtless covered during this first teaching period or which are so apparently " tacked on " that there is little hope of interesting the pupils. If the class is to succeed in carrying over its morning problems into an evening gathering, it will require more stimulating materials in connection with the regular church-school programs than have so far been available. It will also require skill and earnest preparation by teacher and pupils. When the first session has developed a " hot point " of discussion there should be more enthusiasm for the second hour than for the first. But, taken throughout a series of weeks, there is grave danger that the evening session will be regarded merely as a time for the " threshing of old straw." Where a thoroughgoing project is the basis for both sessions, this danger will probably disappear.

2. **The evening meeting as a second session of the department.** Most young people's departments do too few things as a unit. In a large church, it is important that the department as a whole carry on an aggressive program in order that there may be a sense of unity among the young people of the parish. In a small church the department may consist of only two or three classes; in such a case it is equally important that significant undertakings be entered upon unitedly by these classes. If for no other reason, it should be favored because it brings the two sexes together in worship, discussion and service. The evening session, therefore, as a phase of the departmental program is one to be highly commended.

The program cannot center around the themes used as the basis of the Sunday morning class session unless all classes are studying similar subjects; this, of course, would rarely be true. Where it does prevail, however, the evening discussion and the related activities may well have this kind of correlation. Discussion is only one phase of the society program, but it is a very important one. In conducting the worship, arranging socials and bearing responsibility for service enterprises, the various classes which constitute the department may take turns in leadership.

3. The society conceived of as a devotional meeting. In several denominations the evening meeting is thought of primarily as an opportunity for the young people to give expression to their religious experiences. It is in this sense as well as in the larger areas an "expressional" opportunity. The name which lingers on in many local units is that of "prayer-meeting"; the name of the committee responsible for the choice of leaders and the general arrangement for Sunday programs is that of the "prayer-meeting committee." But this is not what most Sunday evening meetings are, especially in those churches where there seems to be the most vitality. And because this is not what they are, and because the idea of a "prayer meeting" brings no great joy to the growing generation any more than it does to their parents, the name had better be changed — changed to fit both the reality of the situation and the psychology of youth.

The type of meeting which young people need is quite different from that which characterized the earlier years of the society movement. We cannot and should not expect young people to get up, week after week, and give testimonies of their religious experience. If we try to force them to do this, we shall certainly find them giving expression to an experience which they did not have, or saying words which they think we approve but which mean little to them. Now and then, under the right kind of leadership, some personal testimony of this sort will come; but more frequently the expression will be in the form of a question, a problem, a conviction, rather than in that of a personal "experience." There is something both good and bad about this modern fact which we must recognize and accept. On the one hand, it would seem that if people — young and old — no longer can get up in a meeting and tell what the love of God has done for them, religion has lost the personal reality which it had in the days of Paul and of our grandfathers. Perhaps there is truth in this. What the church needs, what Christians need, is religion, religious experience. Part of our program is to develop gradually and in a rational way that kind of worship which will lead young people to give honest testimonies of what they know and have felt, but the way to begin is not by expecting them to stand on their feet each week and say "what I thought you wanted me to say."

There is also a wholesome phase of this modern inability to testify. A vast amount of prayer-meeting talk, adult and youthful, has always been cant. It has had no real relation to life; it has been verbiage and not an honest expression of contrition, desire, moral living, communion with God. It has been an emotional expression which brought a temporary satisfaction to the person who spoke, a satisfaction similar to that which comes from parading one's self before an approving crowd. Where it has been the most real it has grown out of an introspection which has often been too intense. Self-examination is such an intimate matter that it is better that it be not done before the eyes of a company. Any sane program of religious education will now and then bring forth a genuine testimony, a cry of complete helplessness, an expression of convincing religious experience; but the process which invites people to the Sunday evening session with the promise that this is to be an hour given over to this form of oral display is thoroughly uneducational and is based upon a wrong conception of the religious experience.

Closely related to this subject of the devotional character of the evening meeting is the whole matter of the type of topics which should be used. For many years the topics selected by the society organizations were essentially of the prayer-meeting type. The topics have probably improved a good deal during the last ten years, but they are still too far from the experience of young people. This is not entirely the fault of the people who make them, for these conscientious leaders labor diligently in an effort to build a set which will meet the desires and needs of the varied types of local leaders in their constituencies. Perhaps no group of persons could succeed any better in creating a list of topics which the many constituent bodies would accept than that group of men and women who prepare the annual lists for the Interdenominational Young People's Commission. Having said this, it cannot be denied that too many of the topics continue to sound like sermon subjects and posit a religious understanding and experience and theological background which the young people simply do not have. What happens when these topics go to the local units?

The young person who is called upon to conduct the meeting has a paucity of information, is moved by high intention to do what he ought to do, and therefore conducts the meeting in the approved fashion; that is, he relies solely upon the printed materials supplied by denominational or interdenominational headquarters. And what does he find there? Considerable material, usually prepared by very busy men and women who write these topical suggestions at breakneck speed during an interlude between their regular pastoral or professional duties. The material itself is usually in terms of adult experience; the approach is seldom educational or natural. The " clipping reading " habit is not to be blamed entirely upon sluggish local leaders. The type of topics has made it almost compulsory. The type of material provided by topical writers has encouraged it. The tradition of past days in the home church has supported it. The devotional meeting, therefore, stays on the low level of reading somebody else's statement about something which has never meant anything to the young people and will not mean much to them tomorrow.

Let no one misunderstand the criticisms of this section. We believe that worship is one of the fundamental phases of the society program. We feel sure that one of the duties of modern religious education is to develop the practice of private devotions. We are convinced that young people need to do more than talk about religion; that they must be led into a natural experience of religion. We believe that they should be given the opportunity of testifying to what they have experienced and to what they need and to what they believe. We agree that many of the subjects which should consume the discussion of the evening hour should be of a distinctly "spiritual" nature. We believe that young people need sound advice from adults, and that they must rely upon the printed helps which competent Christian educators prepare. But we also believe that none of these things will be satisfactorily attained until the old conception of the evening meeting as a "prayer meeting" goes — for prayer meeting means to the young people a stereotyped program of unrealities just as surely as prayer meeting means to many of the older generation something of a similar character, from which they are delighted to be relieved.

4. **The society thought of as a discussion group.** A common characteristic of the present-day society situation is that the Sunday evening meeting is largely of a discussional nature. It provides, under a succession of young leaders, an opportunity for a free consideration of such problems as are set before the group. This is an advance over the former program of pious-sounding comment upon generic themes instead of upon specific perplexities. But it is not sufficient to think of the society program as being restricted to the Sunday discussion. The meeting of inquiry and debate may be the basis for the entire program, or it may be a significant element in it; but it is not an adequate program in itself. Moreover, most young people's groups will not long succeed if the Sunday meeting proceeds along a single line, be it discussion, worship or of a forum type. There will probably be more sessions given over to discussion than to any other method of learn-

ing and expression. Further suggestion regarding the principles which should guide the discussion are provided in the next chapter.

5. The society as an "expressional agency" for young people. During that period when certain leaders of religious education who believed in the single-organization plan made a terrific onslaught upon the society idea, it was defended by its friends as being "the expressional agency for young people's work." The academic theory upon which this defense was made was an erroneous one. It is absurd to think that, ideally, the morning organization should be the one through which a certain amount of fact and "teaching" is injected into the pupils, and that the evening organization (entirely separate, with different leaders, and pursuing a program independently made) should be the means by which this same fact and teaching would be immediately worked out into life. "No impression without expression" was a favorite slogan among all groups. The defenders of the society program insisted that this separate organization was the logical medium by which the impression could be made permanent — it was the expressional agency that completed the learning process. In fact, whether the theory be absurd or not, it must be admitted that much of the teaching of the class session has been made real only as it became practical and definite and vital through the activities of the society; but it is only accidental that this is so. There are certainly as many cases in which no connection between the two occurred at all. The society is an "expressional agency" in the best meaning of the term. It is also an instructional agency, despite the willingness of the society leaders to disclaim this in an effort to pacify the single-organization advocates and to give a distinctive though not all-inclusive character to the society. So is the class an expressional agency — if it is a teaching medium. For the learning process requires that the two things, teaching and expression, be tied up in one whole. Effective teaching becomes possible only when an expressional opportunity is provided. Expression is not a thing in itself, wholly separate from the discovery and impartation of facts.

What, then, is the difference between the class program and the society program? Theoretically, their functions are not so different. In fact, the less we try to define the distinctive character of each, the better for us. The more both of these agencies give their attention to the need for developing a completeness of Christian experience, using every wise method available, the better for us all. Practically, there is usually a difference. The class is under the leadership of an adult, there are more " regular " teaching sessions, there is not so much control and direction by the young people. But this is becoming less true than it was. It has been found that the adult does not need to monopolize the leadership of the class and that its sessions do not need to be formal. There is no reason why the programs of the class and society should not be very similar. There are churches in which the class program satisfactorily accomplishes all that a society could possibly do. There are other churches, in which it seems impossible to get the young people out to a morning session, in which an enlarged evening program accomplishes all that the class plus the society ever aimed to do. There are many more churches in which it seems wiser that there be two organizations, in which the morning session of teaching is supplemented by certain weekday activities of the class, and in which the society also carries on an aggressive round of instructional and service enterprises — the two not conflicting, both agencies being engaged in the unified process of teaching and serving, their programs having been generally agreed upon through a council, the details of each being worked out by its own officers. This continues to be the wise plan for the larger number of our churches at the present time.

6. The society as an agency for some specialized function. There are in some of our larger churches clubs or fellowships which serve distinctive purposes, and which attract a limited number of the young people. In one church, for example, there are a few who want to spend an evening a week reading good stories. In another community, a similar group has a biweekly book review hour. There are young women's guilds and junior brotherhoods. In small churches as well as large, there have been special missionary societies, organized usually by women interested in promoting the missionary program of the denomination. It is impossible to lay down a rule which will apply generally. It should be said, however, that these separate organizations should not be multiplied; that they should be approved only when it is certain that the agencies already set up cannot fulfill the desired functions equally well.

Some Guiding Principles in Program Building

The same philosophy which determines the construction of a curriculum for the class applies in the building of a society program. In addition, the following suggestions are applicable to the group which corresponds to the society.

1. The program should be locally built. Inasmuch as this emphasis runs throughout the entire volume, nothing additional need be said here, except to point out that for many years most society programs were made in the rarefied atmosphere of secretarial offices in metropolitan skyscrapers.

2. It should be an integral part of the educational plan of the church. Now and then a local or national leader disavows any educational intent for the young people's society. It is insisted that the organization exists for a devotional, evangelistic, or expressional purpose and that it is, therefore, outside of the educational area. No amount of protest of this sort alters the fact that the young people who are at work in the society are being educated by the process. If the program runs counter to the main trend of the church's cultural and training program, these young people are being wrongly educated. If the society ignores the intention and the methodology and the plan of the entire educational scheme, the young people lose the total impact which is possible and at the same time are subjected to an educational influence which is harmful. It is a tragic waste if there is no unity between the Sunday morning and weekday program and that which is conducted by the society.

3. **It should be planned by the young people themselves, with the counsel of responsible adults.** The society's outstanding contribution to the training program of the church has been that it encouraged the initiative and creativity of the young people — within limits. It is their organization. It must be conducted as they want it to be. It must deal with those issues with which they are concerned. Its success or failure must be their own. Superimposition by the adults of the church is as bad as superimposition by organizational officials from the outside. But this cardinal principle must not be accepted without approval also of the one which emphasizes the fact that in this matter, as in all of the life of the church, there should be coöperative endeavor between old and young. The committee on religious education, or that group responsible for the total adolescent program, must not be ignored. Nor should they exclude the young people from their deliberations. The function of the religious education or curriculum committee is not to make programs *for* the young people but to make them *with* young people. The complementary phase of this coöperation is that the society should have an adult counselor, or a committee of counselors, who collaborate in the making of society plans. The proper procedure is for the general committee on religious education to outline the large areas of work specifically adapted to the society

type of organization, and for the executive committee of the society to work out the details of their program.

4. **In building its program, the local society needs to take into account the suggestions of national, community and state fellowships.** If the society is a Christian Endeavor organization, it will give earnest consideration to the plans promoted by the national or district officers, but it should not be bound by them in any detail. Those ideas particularly approved by the denominational departments of religious education should receive the same fair attention.

5. **There must be unity in the society program.** Life is unitary. The educational process is a single one. Discussion, worship and service undertakings must contribute to the enrichment of life as a whole. The worship program must, therefore, be constructed in the light of the discussion schedule and the service goals. The discussion program must not be outlined independently of the "activity" program upon which the young people plan to embark. All phases of the common endeavor need to be worked out together and must be consistent with each other, as well as harmonious with the larger educational scheme of the entire church.

6. **The program must be conceived in terms of vital enterprises.** As in the case of the curriculum of the church-school class, it is important that subjects and books be not considered the determining factors in the construction of a program. Areas of human need and interest are the main consideration. The program must be functional, both in its terminology and in its set-up. The society usually offers the best opportunity for the application of the project idea, because it is less formal in its type of meetings and more flexible in its procedure. The Sunday evening discussion is only one phase of the whole matter, but it is a central one. In the selection of subjects for these meetings, there are at least three methods of approach which are common among societies.

First, there is the method of following a series of unrelated topics. This is the most common method, and has until recently been almost the only practice. Sometimes these topics have just been accepted. This required the least work on the part of the local leader. Frequently, it was not apparent to local workers that any other way was open. While it is our opinion that the unrelated topical procedure is the least satisfactory, because it brings a rapid succession of impressions which will be fleeting because there has been no serious and protracted study of the ramifications of the issues, it is recognized that sometimes this plan seems the only practical one for the time being. Moreover, there are times when this method of choosing topics will be a wholesome change — particularly after the group has spent a long time in some intensive study or on a project which has required strenuous application.

If the society uses this topical method, it should be sure that it selects from available sources those problems which it really wants. An Epworth League or Christian Endeavor society should not confine itself to those topics issued by its national organization. It may well consult the lists which come from all of the various society headquarters, from the denominational leadership, from any other available source, and may then make an eclectic list.

Second, there is the method of having a "monthly emphasis," which applies in the discussion and worship and service fields. Many of the printed lists of topics now follow this plan. December, for example, is designated as "social service" month. Too often this is merely a wooden kind of emphasis which involves nothing very definite in the way of a program. This kind of division is the basis of some denominational schedules. January, for example, is designated as "devotional," largely because the Commission on Worship wants an offering taken. February is "educational" because the colleges must be taken care of in the financial program of the society. March is " world brotherhood " because the foreign-mission cause must be promoted. This is one of the most short-sighted policies which any denomination can undertake. Conceived in the minds of adults, it fails to begin or end with or to consider the normal interests of young life. Prepared in good faith because it is felt that young people need to know about the program of the denomination and need also to support it financially, it is still primarily a promotional scheme and the semi-educational methods proposed for the society do not camouflage the fact that the intent is largely financial. It may, for a time, hold loyal young people, but it does comparatively little to educate them and make them fully religious. Alert young people protest that it is an adult program which seeks to exploit youth for the sake of ecclesiastical " big business."

The preceding paragraph is not intended as a disapproval of the policy of following monthly emphases. It seeks to make the argument that if such emphases are adopted they should begin with the experiences of the young people rather than with the objects which denominational mechanics want promoted. The themes should be conceived in terms of things to be done rather than of ideas to be sloganized.

Third, there is the program which is a series of significant enterprises. In using the word " enterprise " it is not the intention to limit the idea to physical busyness. The undertaking may be essentially an intellectual one. A program of this sort might proceed in September with the intention of " Surveying our Field and Outlining the Season's Work," in October with the idea of " Rallying Our Forces behind the Church." There would be abundant work for the committees to do; the discussions could certainly be built around the practical questions which relate to the local field and to the total church opportunity; the worship would take as its theme the particular aspects of the project upon which the group is working. It is almost certain that if a year's work is built up around a series of such undertakings, some lasting a month and others a quarter, interest will be stimulated, educational fruitage will be forthcoming, and a steady growth in the society will result.

7. **It is well to outline a year's program at a time.** During the summer or in the late spring, the executive committee may well plan the general trend of the year's work, assigning to various committees the corresponding responsibilities. In the early fall would come reports of plans and progress. More detailed arrangements would then be made for the first quarter's activities. Some groups will prefer to outline the annual program to correspond with the calendar year, but increasingly the custom is to make it coincide with the school year.

8. **The details of the program had better be prepared for only a quarter at a time.** It is not a good plan for those societies which proceed on the topic-a-month basis to select discussion themes for a year at a time. If this is done for a quarter only, there is a flexibility which makes place for sudden interests and needs. Societies which use the monthly emphasis plan will find it sufficient to arrange details for a three-month period; those which proceed on the basis of a three-month project or some modification of this arrangement, will discover that they have their hands full in handling a single major problem.

9. **In arranging a year's schedule there should be proper consideration of the several aspects of the work which usually need attention.** The program should not be lopsided. For example, in selecting topics it will be found that most subjects fall roughly under one of three general heads: personal matters, social issues, and those questions which deal with faith or the spiritual life. Each of these three areas of need should find a place in the annual program. The same thing is true of enterprises which immediately concern the local group and those which should reach the wider areas of human life: the one should not be emphasized

at the expense of the other. So, too, the group must never forget that it is a part of the church, and that any plans which it makes must contribute to the total life of the church and must enlarge the service which the local body is able to render to Christ's kingdom generally. A balanced program is essential if we are to develop a sane viewpoint among our young people and are to lead them to a balanced kind of living.

Materials Recommended for Further Study

Davis, Bert H. *Citizenship Ideals for Christian Youth.* International Society of Christian Endeavor.

Hardy, C. D. *Youth and Debating.* International Council of Religious Education. (Christian Quest booklet.)

Leslie, Elmer A. *Acquainting Youth with Christ.* International Society of Christian Endeavor.

Maus, Cynthia P. *Youth and the Church.* Standard Press.

Miller, Catherine A. *The Successful Young People's Society.* Richard R. Smith.

Phelps, Edwin. *The Pathfinder in Church Work with Young People.* Judson Press.

Stock, Harry T. *How to Improve a Young People's Program.* Pilgrim Press.

——. *A Year's Program for Young People.* Pilgrim Press.

For discussion materials, consult the various organizational headquarters; such as The International Society of Christian Endeavor, 41 Mt. Vernon St., Boston, Mass.; The Epworth League, 740 Rush St., Chicago, Ill.; The Epworth League (South), 810 Broadway, Nashville, Tenn.; The Baptist Young People's Union of America, 2328 S. Michigan Ave., Chicago, Ill. The intermediate and senior materials issued by the Epworth League, and the Christian Life Topics issued by the Congregational Education Society (14 Beacon St., Boston, Mass.), are built on a unit plan.

Chapter V

THE LEADER — HIS PREPARATION AND METHOD

THE outlining of a program is a large task, but a program on paper is not a program in fact; the real job remains to be done. A paper curriculum is like a party platform: it is a promise of what may be. Only a continuous and aggressive loyalty of the constituency to the plans projected, under the guidance of conscientious and competent leadership, can make this promise a reality. The next consideration, consequently, has to do with the means by which the work proposed may best be accomplished. Because the Sunday sessions are central to the whole undertaking, the present chapter will deal with preparation for teaching, for conducting the meetings and with methods which may be employed by the leaders. The counsel herein given is directed primarily to the superintendent, teacher, and the adult counselor, who must usually take the initiative in suggesting procedures, even in those organizations which are uniquely the possession and responsibility of the young people themselves.

The success of the program depends largely upon three factors, namely:

1. **The leader.** In the church-school this includes superintendents, teachers, class officers, and members of the council. In the evening meeting it applies to the adult counselor and the members of the executive committee.

Further discussion of the adult's opportunity appears on every page of this chapter. At this point it is sufficient to indicate those characteristics which young people have said are most needed by the adult leader. Out of a long list of requirements suggested by delegates in half a dozen summer conferences, the following stand out as most commonly insisted upon:

Ability to get the adolescents' viewpoint and to sympathize with it even if not in agreement with it.

Genuine interest in every member of the group.

A knowledge of the subject.

Interesting presentation of subject matter.

Genuineness of Christian life and purpose.

Sense of humor.

Good personality.

Conduct of sessions on a basis of general participation by the members of the group.

Regularity in attendance.

Patience.

2. **Hard work.** The person who assumes the leadership of an organization of young people should expect to put time and thought into it. He should be willing to give up personal pleasures and certain other social responsibilities if necessary. This leadership must not be taken on simply as "another extra." It must become a major interest. Church-school and society leaders need to repeat, in Coué fashion, many times a day, for weeks on end, this statement: "There is no more important task in the church, open to laymen, than that of teaching or working with a group of boys or girls."

3. **Variety.** Novelty and variety are not to be sought at the expense of dignity, cumulative educational effect, or solid content. But there is no virtue in monotony. A single-tracked method almost certainly spells failure. Human nature, adult and adolescent, demands that life shall be free from drab sameness and insists upon different approaches and a multiplicity of methods. It is not only legitimate to heed this demand, but sound educational theory requires variety and adaptability in program and approach.

General Preparation of the Leader

A capable leader will make effective instruments of the worst materials. He will adapt any course of study so that the special needs of the pupils may be met. Beginning with the young people rather than with the printed course, he will develop a method which will save the situation. Method is more important than materials, and the personality and interest of the leader is the greatest factor of all. But most churches find it harder to discover the perfect teacher than to secure a faultless course of study.

The most conscientious teachers are often the ones who fear that they are incompetent. A great deal has been written about the failures of church-school teachers. Much of it is true. But in spite of incompetence in the teaching staff, the present generation has come to whatever religious understanding it has largely because of consecration upon the part of parents, pastors, teachers, and adult advisers. If it were a choice between devotion and training, we should choose the former; but such a choice is not necessary. Any leader who wants to develop his technique and knowledge has a world of books at his command. Leadership-training courses are provided by the International Council of Religious Education and by most denominations.

1. The old and the new. The leader today has as his assistants a variety of methods as well as a wealth of materials. He must get rid of the idea that because he was brought up under an old régime with a single method, this same procedure is "good enough for our children."

The tendency of each of most of the new developments is to become standardized and single-tracked. They do not develop common viewpoints and similar products; personality is highly respected and those who graduate from such schools or programs bear the marks of individuality. The product is not standardized, but the method is. The process by which it was sought to produce diversity and creativity has become uniform, and to that degree it has become fixed and inflexible. One of the lamentable tendencies among educators is that of throwing overboard the old methods and aids in their devotion to the new. Such a policy is unscientific, short-sighted, and educationally unsound. Soon another new method is discovered and the devotees of that which was novel yesterday become the conservatives of today; they still hold to the single excellent idea which occupied public attention in its heyday. Leaders will find that there are too few new methods even after they have taken into account all our modern developments. They will discover that in their difficult task they need all of the wisdom and experience which has been accumulated through the varied methods of the generations.

Don't throw away old

2. The unique opportunity of the church school. The church has been far behind the procession of the public schools. Eventually, ideas which fight for admittance to the schools are adopted by the church. Long after the label of approval has been placed upon them by general education, the church reticently and ineffectively makes them her own. Religious education is ready to adopt an idea about the time that the schools are ready to drop it, or to push it into a subordinate place.

It need not be so. The church, it is true, is hedged about by all sorts of difficulties. There are conservative laymen, untrained teachers, penurious treasurers, denominational taboos and insistences. But, after all, the local church is its own master. Let it once feel the force of that idea and it will march stalwartly. The teacher in the class can usually direct the program of that class without interference, so long as he is a respected Christian character and is "making a go of it." Like people generally, the church officers want to see success, and the kind of success that they want to see is statistical. This is, of course, a low standard of measurement, but the existence of such a test does not handicap the teacher at the point of trying new methods; for usually it will develop that new methods produce heightened interest, regularity of attendance, numerical growth. Meanwhile it is more likely than not that life results are also accumulating.

The church-school teacher is free from certain handicaps which tie the hands of public-school teachers. The sessions of the classes need not be formal. The students are not required to pass examinations in factual details in order to be graduated into a higher grade, and then to answer all manner of nice questions in order to secure the certificates which entitle them to be teachers or electrical engineers. Most churches attest this comparative freedom of the church-school teacher, in the fact that the average graduate of the senior department has practically no knowledge of Biblical content or of the meaning of Christianity. The lack of standardized requirements has produced this chaos, this inefficiency. The same lack of cut-and-dried system leaves the individual teacher free to introduce any method he desires, if it is a method which will be efficient both in "holding the young people" and in helping them to build Christian character. Let the churches once resolve to be pioneers in education, and they can outpace the school system. But it all depends upon the readiness of the individual leader to march forward in the procession.

3. A carefully selected library. Even the very small school should build up a library, adding systematically to it each year. Ten or fifteen dollars invested annually in the right books will work a great change in the small church. An institution which has an annual budget of five thousand dollars should have an item of at least fifty dollars for this necessary equipment for the teaching force. In addition to books and the teaching materials with which instructors are supplied, several of the best periodicals in the field of religious education should be available. No church should confine its subscriptions to those magazines published by

its own denomination, and certainly no church should be without its denominational helps.

4. The teachers' meeting. The simplest use that can be made of the library is for each teacher, in turn, to read the volumes, digest them and then discuss them with others. This should be the minimum expectation. A regular teachers' meeting may grow out of this simpler beginning. The discussions in these sessions may be based upon, — concrete cases which are met Sunday after Sunday in the classes, the principles and methods expounded in textbooks, the lines of development most needed in the school. A dozen such meetings a year, skillfully led and carefully planned for, should be one of the most energizing factors in the life of the church.

5. Standard training courses. After a time, if not at first, these teachers' meetings should result in standard training courses, to be carried on within a single church or on a community basis. They involve a serious study of the best textbooks; a genuine piece of educational work must be done. Some form of test or examination is required in order that proper credits may be secured. Full information regarding these courses may be secured from the educational officers of the denominations or from the International Council of Religious Education. If a standard course is not desired, various other methods of training leaders are provided by the national offices.

6. Summer conferences. There is, at present, no single agency which offers so much hope for the future leadership of our churches as the summer conference. Hundreds of these gatherings are conducted each year by the various communions, by interdenominational bodies, and by organizations with specialized fields of religious or character education. Tens of thousands of young people of high school age and above are enrolled; camps conducted by local churches and by semi-religious organizations enlist hosts of intermediates; leadership training schools provide high-grade instruction for teachers and adult counselors. The fact is, there are so many of these summer schools that the pastor and his advisers find difficulty in choosing among them. The following suggestions are offered as considerations which may help determine the decisions as to who should go, where they ought to go, and what should be expected of those sent.

Only those should go who have real leadership potentialities.

They should go as representatives of the church.

It is better that at least two or three representatives should go to a given conference.

Full information should be in hand regarding the purposes of the respective conferences. The choice between them should be on an intelligent basis. Organizational loyalty and historical considerations are not the only determining factors. Such questions as the following will naturally be considered:

Will this conference provide those inspirational features which give vision and resolution to these potential leaders?

Is the program thoroughly educational or is it a "pep affair"?

Is the type of training offered of a practical character, making close connection with the local situation?

Is the conference a church gathering? Many camps and assemblies do not have church work specifically in mind; they are conducted by agencies sympathetic to the church but not a part of it. They are valuable. But if the purpose is to train leaders for the program of the churches, those conferences officially related to the church should have first consideration.

Is this an elementary, a standard or an advanced conference? Which gathering should be attended will depend upon the stage of development which the local leaders have reached.

Decisions should not be made solely in terms of a single year.

7. Conventions, institutes, and similar short-period gatherings during the regular "working year." In addition to the summer gatherings and the church or community training courses, local groups are urged to send teachers and young leaders to a variety of county, district, state and national gatherings. The promotional machinery set up to advertise these meetings is frequently very efficient, and insistent appeals are made to the pastor on the basis of loyalty, of great inspirational value, of traditional affiliation, etc. Such pleas must be subjected to sympathetic but critical consideration. Out of such gatherings sometimes come great life decisions and programs of personal and group activity which could not be secured in any other way. Leaders have gone to such conferences and have had their horizons widened and their efficiency increased. A company of adults or young people, unable to attend summer conferences, have had a taste of what the summer gathering provides and have, in consequence, changed the whole character of local work. In deciding among the various gatherings, the same kind of questions should be asked as are listed in the section on summer conferences.

A great deal of money has been unwisely spent in sending leaders a long distance to stirring conventions which have moved their emotions, made some substantial contribution to the thought content, and increased organizational loyalty and efficiency. It is wholly a question of comparative value. The money has not been thrown away, but often it might have been more economically used by sending more leaders to an institute much nearer home. Mass meetings are not the best investment for delegates, except in cases where the main need seems to be to subject the local leader to the awakening which may come from an inspirational address. Institutes, training conferences and schools of methods nearer home, conducted under the leadership of educational experts, are more worthy of support, provided they combine the inspirational and the instructional, and present theories in terms of actual home situations.

A Particular Leader and His Group

1. Advance preparation. Were it not so common for leaders to prepare their outlines on the way to the class or society or even after they arrive, it would be unnecessary even to mention the importance of careful home study. It is not sufficient to read over the paragraphs in the leader's guide so as to be "a jump ahead of the group."

Preparation should begin early in the week. Having read the material provided, the leader will realize that much of it is unfitted for his purpose, some of it is excellent, still other items will need to be reworded, made more concrete, or put into the form of questions or problems. He will understand that before this subject can be adequately handled it must become *his* lesson or topic. He will need to make his own outline. He will need to call up members of the group, assigning to them various problems and questions to think over as the basis for class or society discussion.

From the beginning of the week the matter will be on his mind. From what he reads in the papers and magazines, from what he finds in the neighborhood experiences, from the contacts which he has with young life during the week, a wealth of items will be drawn into his consciousness as by a magnet. At the end of the week he will discover that a mass of pertinent material has accumulated. It is all grist for his mill, because he began his preparation early and kept the class or society session in mind throughout the week.

2. Using local situations. Regardless of good intentions and demonstrated ability, the writers of helps are usually unable to provide illustrations, cases, and comments full of local color or flavor. Even when the materials included are typical of the experience of the race, they generally lack a specificity which makes the best contact with the student mind. A leader will often receive his cue from the printed page, but will make his introduction of the problem in terms of something which he knows has happened in the community, of something that occurred recently and received wide publicity. For example, the lesson that is set for the day may have to do with the problems centering around the idea of success. The textbook would give a number of hypothetical situations. But if this question were being studied during the time when a "Red" Grange is facing the decision between leaving college in order to make a fabulous wealth and staying in school to complete his course, it is very evident that this would prove the best imaginable starting point for the leader.

3. Knowing the group. The leader, like the minister, should not prepare a discourse or a program for people in general, but for a definite group, made up of very definite personalities. The ten boys with whom the teacher meets each Sunday constitute his major interest. The ten together have certain common desires and needs. Each of the ten is different from the others. The lesson period — a precious half hour a week — gives an opportunity for skillful direction, and the individuals are to be thought of in preparation as much as the group as a whole. The teacher must be well acquainted with the daily round of experience in the life of each boy. What a commentary upon a teacher who replies, "I don't know whether Frank is in school or working in a store." It is usually a serious error to use many illustrations from high-school life, if the majority of the boys are earning their living, and probably have a sense of being cheated out of some of life's supposedly free opportunities.

4. Sympathizing with youthful ambitions and foibles. It is not enough to know what happens in the lives of boys and girls. Too often such knowledge has been the foundation for scolding, lecturing, and final estrangement. The adult will not always agree with the ideas that boys hold. He will often wish that it were possible to change them suddenly. He will undoubtedly map out a program by which less worthy ambitions will eventually make way for nobler ideals. But the first step in bringing this to pass is to understand why these ideas are held, why certain habits have been formed. The adult will try to think back to his adolescent days, but he will need also to understand the serious social changes which are so rapidly being brought about. Although he may rebel against these upheavals and though it may be clearly his duty to try to keep his young people from being overwhelmed by modern developments, he must first bring himself to an understanding of what has caused the social shifts and of why young people are susceptible to them. When the young people become convinced that he is a friend to be trusted — no "kill joy," no "old fogey" — they will respond in mind and heart to his reasoned judgments. It is not always certain that the desired life habits will follow, but it is certain that they will not follow unless this sympathetic relationship has first been established.

5. Formulating a specific aim. In thinking ahead to a particular session, the leader will discover a specific purpose for the lesson or topic. It is not enough to "cover the ground," to "teach what the theme indicates." If the Biblical text has no obvious application for this group, something should be substituted; the time available during a year is so limited that a leader cannot afford to waste a single period on an insignificant issue. There are too many serious problems in adolescent experiences; vital substitutions are always possible. Usually, however, the lesson or topic has in it the kernel of a practical emphasis. Suppose, for example, that the first chapter of Genesis is the assigned Bible passage. What shall be the main purpose of the teaching? Shall it be to show that at the heart of the universe there is a good God, to indicate the peculiar position of man in the order of the universe, explain the value of the chapter in the light of modern scientific discoveries? Manifestly, a brief lesson period will not allow for adequate emphasis on all three of these large matters.

The leader will have to decide, early in the week, what the most significant emphasis is for the particular group with whom he meets. It would not be the same for the intermediate and senior ages, for students in a first-class high school and for boys who never went beyond the eighth grade.

6. Letting the discussion take its course. It is the leader's business to have at least a mental outline of the hour's probable discussion, but he should not be troubled if this plan is sidetracked for something apparently more important. He should respect it enough to insist upon keeping to the main line, if irrelevant or trivial matters come up; but if some one introduces a problem which is closely related to immediate needs, it is better to forget the outline and to see the issue through to a satisfactory conclusion.

The leader's notes, lectures and general plans are means to an end. He should be very happy if some better method for the accomplishment of that end is suggested by the young people. It is a healthy sign when a group is so concerned about an issue that the solution is not found and agreed upon during a single session. He is a wise counselor who is willing to disarrange next week's schedule in order that the discussion of this week may be carried nearer its conclusion.

7. The attitude of a learner. The adult will go to the class hoping that he will furnish certain information and guidance to his less mature comrades. He will hope also that these young people will be led out into discussion so that they will help each other. But he makes a great mistake unless he, too, expects to learn from them. No person is equipped for leading a group of wide-awake young people unless he is open-minded and ready to grow with them. All members of the company meet from week to week in the double rôle of learner and teacher.

8. The wisdom of experience. Young people, as a rule, will recognize the superior wisdom of adult leaders if these leaders themselves do not insist, in word or attitude, that they are superior. They will not defer to age, in the abstract; but they will hold in high regard the judgment of a particular adult whom they have come to honor and love. They need to understand that experience teaches many things; that from their present position alone they are unable to decide wisely many of the major perplexities of life, or to form adequate philosophical or ethical judgments. It is true also that age alone does not insure wisdom, that wider experience does not always result in a broadened mind and an enlarged horizon. Many young people are far ahead of their leaders. Some of them know it. That is one reason that the church-school class seems to them so hopelessly passé. It is only in the attitude of being humble and eager fellow seekers for truth that an adult and a group of young people can make genuine progress toward the larger life.

Methods of Instruction

1. **Teaching by exposition.** Perhaps the most common practice in church-school classes has been that of " reading around " — each member of the class reading a verse of Scripture, comment upon these verses being made either as each is read or at the close of the entire passage. The comment is seldom original or very pertinent. Occasionally the students are asked to give their opinions of the implications of the verses. Topical or lesson materials which are built upon this plan seldom have the youthful viewpoint. They are more concerned with fine points of interpretation than with the realities of young life. It is a killing process — the teacher holds on longer than the pupils do.

2. **Teaching by the lecture method.** Another common practice is that by which the class goes into a period of preaching or exhortation. The similar society procedure is that of having a procession of outside speakers. The adult is the active participant, the young people are there as listeners. The degree of pas-

sivity is often very high. The amount of restlessness is equally great. The idea is that there is something of value which the leader must impart to the immature or the ill-informed. The function of the pupils is to learn, but this is not the way in which young people learn most readily; indeed, there are those who assert that a person never learns simply by listening. This is probably an exaggerated viewpoint, but it is safe to say that teachers who proceed entirely on this basis are usually not more than twenty-five per cent efficient, and that societies that have no more active program than this probably have hardening of the arteries.

There are occasions upon which the lecture method is useful. For example, it has been discovered that at certain times young people want to listen, that there are some subjects regarding which they do not want to open their minds to others. An attempt at a sorority house, by a visiting leader, to conduct an afternoon session on the discussion basis was frustrated by the complete silence of the group and the insistence of the president that the visitor should give an address. Later, the reason was disclosed to a local worker. These students did not know the guest who had been "wished" upon them. They knew nothing of his sympathies, prejudices, or abilities. Consequently, "We weren't going to bare our minds to him, so that he could go around to another campus and tell students there what we are thinking about." These same girls, with a local trusted adult, would have rebelled at being preached to when there were so many matters that they really wanted to discuss.

One sometimes finds a group of high-school students who voluntarily ask that their class shall study a particular book of the Bible. For months they have been considering "practical problems." Suddenly, they awake to the fact that they know nothing about the Bible even though they were supposed to have studied it for years. Of their own volition they insist on "studying the Bible." They have become an "interest group." For a quarter or more they will maintain a keen interest in that portion of the Bible that they have chosen. Even the expository method may hold them, and they will listen to the lectures of their pastor, whereas they would have objected to "being lectured to" a few months earlier. The reason for the changed attitude is that a compelling interest has dictated their choice. But under normal conditions, with ordinary leaders and ordinary young people, we cannot take it for granted that they will have a consuming interest in the text of the Bible itself, as the main content material of a departmental program. And that being true, it is usually necessary for a leader to adopt some more attractive method than the lecture plan. For most of us are not interesting lecturers. Our boys and girls do not like to hear us preach or exhort as much as we do ourselves.

3. **Teaching through the forum.** The forum is the lecture method with the most objectionable features eliminated. It is more useful for larger groups and at evening sessions than at a Sunday class meeting, unless there is more time available than is usually the case. If an hour is available, half of it may be used in the presentation of the talk and the other half in questions and discussion. A group of older students may add greatly to their knowledge by inviting a succession of specialists to come into the class on consecutive Sundays, the understanding being that they shall speak directly to a given point, and that the class will expect answers to their queries. There are some subjects upon which the local leader feels poorly informed. His opportunity for securing first-hand information is limited. There is no book which handles the entire subject in such a way that he can pass on its contents to the class. A dozen specialists on specific issues will often be able to cover the ground effectively.

The forum method is not recommended as the normal procedure for most groups; certainly it is not the one for intermediates, and even seniors should use it sparingly. It appeals to many minds because it offers the allurement of hearing a variety of speakers, thus breaking that monotony of leadership which seems to irk both old and young in these restless days. As an occasional element in the program — say, for one quarter during a year — it may serve a unique purpose, especially in older groups; but it provides too little participation by the young people themselves. Sharing in discussion is not enough; research before the discussion is needed, and an energetic program growing out of it is important. Decisions are too often made and attitudes established upon some superficial basis, such as the fluency or halting manner of speech, the organizational relationships of the guest, or a comparison with those who have come before and those who follow. Moreover, we need to beware of all methods which tend to make us mere rooters in the grandstand.

4. Teaching through the question box. No outline of courses or set of topics actually reaches all the specific questions which tempt or baffle the minds of young people. Nor does skillful teaching or the forum method make sure that the members of the group will fully reveal their innermost perplexities. They want to ask their questions without having it known that they are asking them. They want sympathetic answers which are neither dogmatic nor hesitating. The question box has been found a useful means by which the need may be met, provided the adult is competent to supply information and tactful in his approach.

It may be used in several ways: a series of discussions by the regular teacher or by the pastor, during a quarter or six weeks, based upon questions handed in by the young people; one night a month given over to the discussion of a number of questions which have been left in the box; a brief series of " one question each Sunday " features as a ten-minute phase of the morning school worship or as a special element in the evening meeting. Better results can be gained if the young people are asked not to sign their names to the queries placed in the box. Sometimes the group will want to participate in the discussion; at other times they prefer to be receptive, feeling that they have asked for information and that it is the adult's function to supply it.

5. **Teaching through dramatics.** What we see is likely to make a deeper impression upon us than what we hear. An imaginative or dramatic production has an appeal which a mere factual presentation does not have. When one participates in the rôles of a drama the impression is still deeper, and when one shares in the creation of the lines or the plot it is most effective of all. "The method teaches in a concrete way; it presents examples for imitation; ideals are formed; great personalities serve as a type of moral ideal, thus giving a human and vital form to the concept of noble living."[1] In planning a quarter's work, it will often be discovered that there are certain natural points at which the dramatic method may be effectively used. If the program has to do with the outlook of the church, some of the local, national or international situations which the church is trying to meet may be pictured. In the process of securing the necessary facts for this production the young people will have learned more, and learned it more completely, than if books had been read without any more specific purpose than to get facts, or to conduct discussions in keeping with a printed program. Sunday evenings may be given over, now and then, to the presentation of a powerful play. Sometimes, where it seems unwise to prepare a finished dramatization, it will be found helpful to read together one of the outstanding productions which are aimed at the level of the young people's intelligence and interest.

6. **The use of stories.** Intermediates often find it difficult to enter intelligently into discussion, but they are intensely inter-

[1] From "Youth and Dramatics," by Grace Sloan Overton, p. 8. (Christian Quest pamphlet.) Copyright, International Council of Religious Education. Used by permission.

ested in stories suited to their " grown-up estate." Stories prepared for juniors will not do! Seniors and young people are also interested in fiction, biography and historical sketches. The church school has a vast amount of story material to draw upon: the missionary enterprise, the chronicles of Christian history, incidents and " cases " which will help to guide young people in meeting aright their daily life situations. Much of the very best material of this sort was not prepared primarily for this purpose and is not listed as " Sunday school material." It is just good literature, with a high moral tone.

The story may be used as an element in a morning teaching or worship period, it may be an illustration in the teaching of a particular lesson, it may be the point of departure from which the entire discussion takes direction, or it is possible just to read a good story together; it is then the sole element in the teaching period. Helpful variety will be brought into the evening meetings by an occasional session which is of the story-reading character. This informal type of program, with young people seated in a circle or around a fire, is often much more effective than the discussion meeting with chairs in " regular " fashion.

7. The discussion method. Discussion is the favorite method in groups of young people today. In the evening meeting, the young people usually lead, and they themselves guide the direc tion of the thought and participation. Sometimes they ask th adult to sum up the conclusions at the end; sometimes they ex pect him to " straighten them out " at various points during th meeting. There are various conceptions of the function of th adult, ranging all the way from the idea that he is largely " re source material," to be drawn upon only when the young peopl ask for information, to the opinion that he should step in fre quently in order to bring the participants back to the main track Two things must constantly be kept in mind during the evenin session: the meeting belongs to the young people and they mu have freedom of thought and action and must not be handicapped by the eager desire of the adult that right conclusions should be reached suddenly; and secondly, the adult should be so thoroughly a member of the group that when he firmly believes that a hint of their wandering or lack of perspective should be given, he will feel free to give it. In the class session, the same freedom of discussion will be followed, but the adult will be much more responsible for introducing the main points, for bringing the thought back to the central issues, for suggesting ideas which have not occurred to the young people, and for summing up the matters of common opinion and of disagreement.

In class or society, the function of the adult leader is that of guide and counselor. He is a member of the group and joins with the others in the double rôle of learning and teaching. He must be open-minded; he must respect the opinions of others. He should not monopolize the time; he will be more successful if he does only enough talking to draw out the young people themselves, to set them thinking, to guide them along the salient lines, to suggest considerations not apparent, and to help them to come to reasonable conclusions. He should offer his opinions when asked for them, but there should be no dogmatism or finality in his attitude. Unless some young person can do it better, he should be responsible for summarizing the day's discussion and for indicating the connection with the next week's program.

"It is customary for societies and clubs to have at least one adult counselor. He will be in the background, although his opinion should frequently be sought by the young people. With younger groups he will be expected to take more initiative, offering suggestions more freely and giving more minute attention to details of planning. It is wise for the adult to do most of his work before the meeting. His great opportunity is that of coaching the leader; if he is prominent during the discussion period he may embarrass the person in charge, and it is likely that many of the members will feel under restraint. In helping the leader to plan the meeting, he should not try to predetermine the trend of the argument, nor should he relieve the leader of the responsibility of outlining the major items of the program. He may point out alternatives, indicating various issues which may come up and which need to be watched, prepared for, and guided. His function is that of showing the leader how he may prepare.

" There are at least four weaknesses in discussions as carried on in our young people's groups. The first is lack of preparation. There is no excuse for this, if the leader is ' on the job ' early and if the material is made available to the group.

"The second weakness appears when every one talks about everything without knowing very much about anything. Frequently, the reason is that the subjects under consideration are beyond the range of present experience.

" It is true, in the third place, that many discussions do not ' arrive '; time is wasted over side issues; the meeting degenerates into controversy over small matters. The leader should hold the participants to the main issue. Secondary matters should be noted on the blackboard in a separate column; these may be referred to later if there is time, or they may form the topics for other sessions. Make a careful use of the blackboard in all meetings. The summary at the close should help the group ' to arrive ' — not that they will always agree, but that the issues should be clear enough for each person to make his own decisions intelligently.

" The fourth weakness is that so often ' nothing happens ' after the meeting. Discussion is good mental exercise, but the purpose of a class or society session goes beyond that. The idea is to help build up Christian character and to secure right social action. Discussion which comes in naturally as a part of a project is more vital than discussion which is an end in itself. But even where the group is not engaged in a project covering study and activity extending over several weeks, it is possible to have definit practical results from the meeting; and this should always be expected. A project may grow out of a discussion as well as involve discussion in its later processes. The value of a meeting is proved when, as a result of it, something worth while happens!"[2]

Materials Recommended for Further Study

Betts, George H. *How to Teach Religion.* Abingdon Press.

Betts, George H. and Hawthorne, Marion O. *Method in Teaching Religion.* Abingdon Press.

Elliott, Harrison S. *The Process of Group Thinking.* Association Press.

——. *The Why and How of Group Discussion.* Association Press.

Gregg, Abel J. *Group Leaders and Boy Character.* Association Press,

Kilpatrick, William H. *Foundations of Method.* Macmillan.

Maus, Cynthia P. *Youth and Story-Telling.* International Council of Religious Education. (Christian Quest booklet.)

——. *Teaching the Youth of the Church.* Doubleday, Doran.

Myers, A. J. W. *Teaching Religion.* Westminster Press.

Miller, Elizabeth E. *Dramatization in the Church School.* University of Chicago Press.

Overton, Grace S. *Drama in Education.* Century.

——. *Youth and Dramatics.* International Council of Religious Education. (Christian Quest booklet.)

Raine, James W. *Bible Dramatics.* Century.

Shaver, Erwin L. *How to Teach Seniors.* Pilgrim Press.

——. *The Project Principle in Religious Education.* University of Chicago Press.

Sheffield, Alfred D. *Training for Group Experience.* The Inquiry.

Sheridan, Harold J. and White, G. C. *Learning and Teaching.* Methodist Book Concern.

Slattery, Margaret. *You Can Learn to Teach.* Pilgrim Press.

Smith, Frank W. *Leaders of Young People.* Methodist Book Concern

St. John, Edward P. *Stories and Story-Telling.* Pilgrim Press.

Suter, John W. *Creative Teaching.* Macmillan.

[2] From *Christian Life Problems,* by Harry Thomas Stock, p. 6 ff. Pilgrim Press.

Watson, Goodwin B. and Gladys H. *Case Studies for Teachers of Religion.* Association Press.

Weigle, Luther A. *The Pupil and The Teacher.* Pilgrim Press.

How a Leader Proceeds with a Group. International Council of Religious Education. (Christian Quest booklet.)

How to Study Individual Growth. International Council of Religious Education. (Christian Quest booklet.)

Religious Education, (magazine), October 1926.

Chapter VI

WORSHIP

IT is still true that comparatively few schools and societies have well-prepared periods of worship. Too often it is supposed that hymns, prayers and Scripture will take care of themselves. The first few minutes are considered as "opening exercises" which give the leader a chance to catch up with himself in preparing for matters which ought to have been attended to hours before, and to give late-comers a chance to trail in. As long as this is true there will be little training in worship and that little will be of the wrong type. If the teaching of the lesson is a major consideration, the service of praise and prayer and aspiration and resolution is equally important. If preparation is required for an intelligent discussion, careful and extensive preparation is needed if the personal attitudes and the group atmosphere are to be most congenial for the teaching or discussion.

Both in the morning session of the church school and in the evening society or club meeting, provision should be made for a fifteen or twenty minute worship service. This should be a unit in itself, complete and separate. There should be no breaks, interruptions, incongruities. All announcements should be kept out of this service. All frivolity should be avoided. There should be no whispering or consultation on the part of leaders. All details ought to be so completely arranged that there are no loose ends requiring last minute attention. Worship is an art; a slight flaw may spoil the entire effect. The period of worship should prepare the heart and mind and will for that resolution which it is hoped will result from the teaching and discussion. Seed will sprout best in soil which is fertile and prepared for planting. The worship session should do that for the human soil and for the words to be spoken during the period of instruction.

Some educators tell us that it is wrong to provide set forms of worship, that we do violence to real educational values by attempting to induce certain emotional states. They say that if there is to be audible prayer, it must always come in the midst of a discussion when the group has reached the point of being particularly grateful, or recognizing an impasse, or of having reached an intellectual conclusion. Spoken prayer, therefore, becomes an emergency matter. But should not Christian prayer be an aid in determining the direction of the discussion? Is there not great personal value in worship for its own sake, aside from the strictly utilitarian aspects? It is contended that a good piece of writing or sweeping or mining is as truly a prayer as a spoken petition or a hymn sung in praise. All discussion is prayer, according to this definition, and perhaps this is the only prayer that is needed. This is both a Christian and a correct psychological view — as far as it goes.

But it is a mistake to maintain that people are moved primarily by uncolored reason, that we must appeal to the rational faculties alone. Those who believe that we must simply allow facts to speak for themselves, and that young people will immediately act upon the facts as presented to them and as apprehended by their minds, do not know human nature. Now, as in Paul's day, we may know the right and yet lack the power to do it. It is not mental power alone that we lack; it is the right emotional power, or the right direction of the emotions. We need a resource greater than we possess. Young people act in keeping with the impulse of the moment. They yield to emotional pulls rather than to reason argument, intellectual decision. The fact that there has been a service of worship may not restrain them or determine a positi wholesome course; but if worship is repeated week after week, the likelihood is that there will be an accretion to their spiritual power which will ultimately enable them to make their muscles obey their minds. Such an effective worship service must have reality, and its technique and content must be the result of assiduous preparation.

No education is adequate which does not help to create the right kind of emotional states. Christianity certainly deals as much with heart-pulls and passions as it does with opinions and judgments. The spiritual resources which human beings need cannot be created simply by discussion and cold reasoning. Part of the process of building strong Christian life involves reading, meditation, music, appreciation of beauty of color and form, common participation in praise and gratitude and quiet. The new rationalism is, of course, a reaction against the wild and dangerous emotionalism which has sometimes degraded American protestantism. We have created states by which the heart wholly ruled the head, to the extent even of causing the mind to abdicate. All sorts of sins have been committed as a consequence. Religion has been brought into disrepute. An emotional debauch has resulted which has dissipated both body and soul. But the cure for this excess and intoxication is not to do away with worship and private devotions. It is not to ignore the affectional side of our beings. We leave the life bare and crippled unless there is training of the appreciative, the impulsive and the volitional faculties.

Is the attempt to create emotional states an effort to interfere with the natural unfolding of life? Can we conscientiously advocate the imposition of emotional attitudes when we are opposed to any effort which will lead the group to make intellectual decisions for an individual? Well, one may ask, what is the function of the Christian church in a world where the forces of evil have preempted the right of way, in which colorful and enticingly beautiful allurements beckon the life-loving youth from every side? Has the church any function which will permit it to suggest to young life that there is still a God in the world, that this God is able and ready to provide lasting and satisfying inner experiences beyond comparison with the fleeting pleasures of those who live by the impulse of the moment? Do democracy and freedom and self-expression mean that we shall simply allow our youth to be exposed to every evil and unlovely influence in life, and then trust the good God to save them from going wrong, without any effort of ours to keep their hearts from bondage to pleasure, self-satisfaction and the lower ambitions? Has self-expression become the whole philosophy of life, or is there still place for the idea of self-control? If there is need of self-control, we must summon all the available resources of heart and mind and will. Talk will not create these resources or summon them to our aid. Activity alone is not sufficient. We need still that reaching out to the great God who is a source of beauty and power and goodness. We need that reaching out in times of calm as well as during seasons of stress; when there is no emergency, in the hope that some of the rude emergencies of life may be avoided. Worship is still one of the potent instrumentalities within the use of the church, and we have not begun to make wise or adequate use of it.

Elements of Worship

1. Prayer. The spirit of prayer is that in which worship should be conducted. This is not to say that a mood of funereal solemnity should overhang the group; quite the contrary — a spirit of joyful appreciation and praise should prevail. Nor is there any contradiction between the scientific attitude and the reverent spirit. The prayerful attitude is wholly consistent with an eagerness to learn. The rationalizing faculties are not asleep during worship. Communion with God is not an opiate, nor is it realized best when the intelligence has been lulled to sleep. But the worship period is not essentially an analytical, an argumentative, or a didactic session. It is a time during which the group approaches God in the attitude of confident friendship and yet of humble adoration, in the hope that immediate joy and satisfaction may be found and that clarity of purpose and strength of resolution for the future may be attained. It is desirable that this same spirit of worship shall be carried over into the humdrum moments of daily living. It is a "spirit of life" that we seek to develop in a growing generation. But as there are times of special intellectual application, so there are legitimately times of deep spiritual communion. During moments of analytical study one does not divorce himself from those spiritual qualities which make him a lovable human being. In time of intensive communion, he does not do violence to his rational faculties.

First, young people need to understand the meaning of prayer. It is a subject which perplexes them greatly. They say prayers and think prayers; yet they have doubts regarding the necessity of prayer, its effectiveness and reality in a world of science. And the reason is that they seldom understand what prayer is. To most of them it is a "give-me" process. It is an emergency matter — a call for help, an attempt to protect themselves or others against feared eventualities, a precaution in the face of unpleasant possibilities. Our first task, therefore, is to introduce them to an experience of genuine prayer, and to provide instruction in its meaning. Prayer has been defined as "communion with God." It is as much listening for God as it is talking with him. It is grounded in appreciation, it finds its first expression in gratitude, it becomes increasingly real as a sense of friendship and fellowship with God develops, it cries out in indignation against injustice and evil, it seeks mercy and succor for those in distress, and it asks that assistance for personal needs which present problems demand. But it is essentially awareness of God, with a resulting deepened desire for things noble and benevolent.

Second, they need the assistance of helpful devotional materials. A good book of devotional literature, prepared by worshipful Christians with young people especially in mind, is a necessary aid to an understanding of the meaning of prayer. Adolescents may be introduced to such helps by the wise use of such materials in connection with the Sunday services, by the study of such literature as a part of the class curriculum, and by a planned group practice of reading daily portions from this book.

Third, they need that demonstration by adults which will make them feel the power of prayer. In this regard the churches have failed lamentably. The confession of a group of high-school people that "we have learned to pray better when our pastor is not present" is a terrific indictment against professional leadership in prayer. The pastor, superintendent or counselor should make detailed preparation of heart and mind, of thought and word, for the public prayer that he is to offer in the presence of the young people. Both in the "preaching service" and in the smaller groups the adult has the opportunity of accomplishing as much through the brief period of audible prayer as he has through the sermon or discussion. Beautiful and impressive though this may be, however, it has no wholesome effect unless the reality of the form is attested by the atmosphere which the adult carries about with him in his daily human contacts.

Fourth, they need training in the habit of public prayer through the practice of prayer itself. On the one hand, it is reasonable to expect the public service of prayer to inspire daily devotional moods, and on the other hand we know that helpful leadership on Sunday depends upon a constantly recurring experience of private prayer: the two things are mutually complementary. For most young people today, the natural process begins with the Sunday service; if they are to find time for an interest in daily prayer habits it will be because the Sunday experience has seemed real and useful. The responsible adults, therefore, must give a planned leadership in the use of various means of prayer. The following are a few of the outstanding forms of prayer which have proved helpful in young people's work:

The adult prayer.
The sentence prayer.
The great prayers of the church.
Biblical prayers.
Prayers written by young people.
Poems which breathe the spirit of prayer.
Hymns as prayers.
Music as prayer.
Silence.
Directed silence.

2. Scripture passages. Care should be exercised in the selection of Biblical material. There are some chapters which are not suited to adolescent worship, because of their irrelevancy, their abstractions, or their unethical emphases. It is not necessary that every idea be wholly transparent to the adolescent, but it is essential that he be able to read the passage as a whole with understanding and conviction. The leader should watch such points as the following:

First, the Scripture passage should be selected because it bears a direct relation to the theme of the service. This will require thoughtful choice in advance of the meeting.

Second, the person who reads the passage should do it effectively. He should be encouraged to take his Bible, close the door of his room, stand before the mirror, and read it aloud several times.

Third, responsive readings are useful. They should not be too heavily depended upon. There is a great deal of day dreaming during most of our responsive services.

Fourth, extra-Biblical material may be drawn upon as supplementary to the Bible verses. Helpful comments from books, poems, excerpts from literature — these are invaluable aids.

3. **Music.** This element consumes more time in the services of worship than any other feature, and involves the entire group in active participation. Consequently, it determines the atmosphere or character of the meeting. The following suggestions may help in planning the musical program:

Jazz and doggerel should be ruled out of worship periods. Those songs which make it easier to dance than to worship, to imagine one's self in a theater than in the house of God, which smack more of sentimental love-verses than of classical poetry, have no place in the worship period.

Songs or hymns which contain unsound ethical ideas or theological crudities should not be used. Worship should be honest and Christian. We do not praise God by singing ideas which we abhor, or which we should abhor.

Hymnals should be of a high order, musically and from the standpoint of literature. The church hymnal is suitable for young people if it is suitable for Christians generally. If the church can afford a separate hymnal, carefully built for adolescents, it will be a good investment; but there is no economy in buying a separate song book for young people, if it is of the trashy sort. If young people seem to insist upon " peppy " songs which contain little religion and less literary and musical character, it is usually because the older people have not trained them in the appreciation of quality.

There should be a reason for the inclusion of every hymn. It must make the right contribution, at the right time, to the worship impression. " Has anybody a hymn he'd like us to sing? " is a question which should rarely, if ever, be asked in a worship service.

The leadership must be inconspicuous and worshipful. The song leader is not a bandmaster or an acrobat. His function is not to create "pep." He is not to call out trick procedures through the use of vaudeville devices or even of "community singing" methods. This does not mean that these measures are bad; it simply means that they do not belong in a service of worship. Anything that detracts from the spirit of communion and which emphasizes the leadership or the methodology is to be avoided.

All special music should harmonize with the general theme of the day and help to heighten or deepen the effect. This should be a matter of careful consultation between the leader and the persons asked to participate in solo or special group rôles.

There should be instruction in the appreciation of hymns and music. This may come about through curriculum elements in the class or society. In summer conferences and similar training schools attention should be given to this matter. The plan of having a "hymn for the month," with explanations of the conditions under which the hymn was written and of its particular value for Christian living, is quite common and wholesome.

4. Talks. Talks are frequently a part of the worship service but they should seldom be regarded as the major element. The person who is to give the talk should understand that his time is very limited, and that his presentation is to relate itself to the theme of the service and to that which precedes and follows. A five- or ten-minute talk in the usual Sunday morning period is all that should be expected.

5. Stories. Stories, well read or told, are often more effective than addresses or sermonettes. Great care should be taken in the selection of materials. "Sob stuff" must be avoided. Better material can sometimes be found in collections of stories not prepared for church-school use than in those books written to teach religious lessons. There is a wealth of missionary material of a high order regarding which denominational offices can give information.

6. Dramatics. Dramatization is one of the popular developments in educational method. It may be used, sparingly, during the worship session as during the period of instruction; for example, the simple portrayal of a Bible event makes a lasting impression. A similar demonstration of a missionary incident, in ten minutes, induces noble attitudes and may produce working plans to be eagerly supported. But such presentation must be carefully prepared, so that there will be no delays or slips or incongruities.

7. Pictures. Just as young people have not usually been led to an appreciation of the values of music, so they know little of art. A new picture, intelligently selected, to be hung in the church may be the center of a worship service. An entire series of worship periods may center around some of the great religious paintings. Prints of some of these most significant works of art may be secured at a low cost.

8. Ritualistic elements. There have been some elements of ritual in most of our young people's organizations, although they have not usually been so considered. The regular repetition of the Mizpah benediction is a case in point; the periodical reading of a pledge, covenant or creed is another. One of the promising developments resulting from a revived interest in worship is the increased use of ritualistic elements.

9. The offering. The offering is an act of worship. It is not so much an item of business as it is the expression of devotion to the cause of Christ. It deserves a place in the period of worship. The announcement regarding it should be simple and reverent, and the tradition should be established that there is no " let-down " when this point in the service is reached. Appropriate music is a great help in maintaining the spirit of worship. (Where the classes take their own collection, it is hardly possible to include the offering as an element of worship.)

Constructing the Worship Program

The building of a beautiful service of worship may be thought of as the work of an architect plus that of a mason: one plans the entire structure around a single great idea, selects those pieces of material which fit into the general scheme, watches eagerly every detail, and rejoices with satisfaction when an artistic and useful structure is completed. It is both a practical task and an artist's fulfillment. It involves scientific selection, utilitarian fashioning. Some seem naturally skilled in the art of shaping an artistic product; others must study and labor and experiment in order to produce that which still shows many signs of poor craftsmanship. We need not despair if we fall short of our ideal. It is inexcusable, however, not to envision a lofty ideal, not to use our talents in a serious endeavor to make real our dream.

1. There must be a central theme. Worship which has no centralizing idea is like a picture without a subject or a musical composition without motif. Immediate spiritual results and lasting moral stimuli depend upon a centrality of aim. Everything that is included in the program must have significance as it relates itself to this theme. The arrangement of the items must be such as to give proportion, cumulative effect, emotional and intellectual climax. There are several ways of selecting themes.

First, the theme may be related to the subject for discussion or study. This is an approved practice which has everything to commend it. So long as schools and societies base their study and discussion upon topics and materials furnished by textbooks and magazines, it is logical to fit the worship emphasis to the content of the study.

Second, the worship program for a month may be built around a central idea. On successive weeks, different phases of the larger theme would be treated. These monthly emphases may be chosen with some thought of correlation with the discussion subjects, or with the idea of presenting throughout the year a series of cardinal interests; such as Christian virtues, the outreach of the church, the elements of Christian faith.

Third, seasonal interests may be taken into account. At the beginning of a church year there is the idea of consecration and loyalty, as the Christmas season approaches the dominant note may be that of devotion to Jesus or of service to humanity, in the summer the minds of young people turn naturally to the God we see in nature.

Fourth, the Sunday services may be related to the daily devotional readings. In some churches, there is a completely outlined plan of daily meditational materials, and the Sunday service would be a natural culmination of the thought of the week.

Fifth, the worship theme may grow out of a project in process. Where regular discussion or study materials are not the basis of the curriculum but the project idea predominates, the worship period from Sunday to Sunday will depend upon the progress of the common enterprise. It will mark the culmination of a particular step in the process, the expression of a sense of gratitude or need.

2. Worship requires serious preparation on the part of the leaders. It is true that many great experiences of worship come spontaneously; but it is not true that in the fifteen- or twenty-minute period on Sundays there will be enough of these great experiences which flash suddenly, without preparation, to justify leaders in making no preparation. God shows himself to human minds and hearts when persons are ready to behold him. The process of preparation is essentially that of enabling young people to see and understand the God who is ever at hand.

First, a responsible committee should be charged with the task of arranging the worship. This may be the executive committee the program committee, a little group of whom the vice-president is chairman. There should be enough capable persons on thi committee so that effective results are assured. While the nucleus of the group may remain the same throughout the year, it is wise to bring in different young people from time to time to deliberate and to plan specific services.

Second, adult assistance is usually desired. Some person who has a " sense of the fitness of things " and who is willing to make this a special interest will be of real help to the young people. He must not be depended upon to furnish most of the ideas, or to do the major part of the work; he is essentially " resource material," upon which the young people may draw.

Third, actual leadership should be distributed among the membership. Timid persons should be given minor rôles at first. It is sometimes wise to have two leaders in the society, one to guide the discussion, the other to conduct the worship. Those who are to be asked to take any place in the program, such as reading the Scripture, should be approached long before the meeting. This will impress the person with a sense of the importance of his contribution, and should lead him to study the passage so as to be able to read it effectively. The main task of the adult is by way of coaching or providing suggestions for the participants before the meeting. He may well take his turn, along with the young people, in conducting the service — this is an evidence of the fact that he is " one of them " and it provides him a good opportunity of demonstrating the niceties of the art of worship leadership.

Fourth, the component parts of the program should be timed so that there is no dragging, with consequent weariness. There is more danger of having too much material than of not having enough, of having ill-planned remarks which consume time and lose the audience. A simple service, planned in every detail and conducted with confidence and order, will create and maintain the spirit of worship much better than a longer and more elaborate one which has its high points of interest and its protracted moments for daydreaming.

3. The aims of worship should always be kept in mind by those who plan the service. There are two types of aims: the immediate result to be accomplished by this particular service, and the underlying objectives of worship as an integral part of the entire religious education program. The following are a few of the desirable results, which, during a period of weeks, may be expected of the worship phase of the curriculum.

First, the young people should be led to a sense of the reality of God. Prayers are directed to God. Scriptural and literary materials should help to reveal the mind of the Father. Musical numbers assist in establishing communion with God. A single experience on a given Sunday, enforced by the repeated periods of succeeding weeks, often has the effect of a Damascus road revelation. Unless the church program of worship succeeds in making God real, it fails of its first intention.

Second, certain informational content should be added to the store of the worshipers. Worship is not primarily an instructional process, but it is a reasonable procedure. Everything that goes into it must have educational merit. The content of worship programs should make easier the understanding of the way of life, and should reënforce the instruction which comes during other sessions.

Third, ideals should be clarified and lifted. Those thoughtful persons who came into contact with Jesus went away with new visions, deeper loyalties to truth, ideals which raised the level of their thinking and living. The experience should not be otherwise in the period of worship, when our eyes behold the Father and our minds contemplate the character of Jesus.

Fourth, resolution and determination should be added to judgments and convictions. The intellectual grasping of truth, the glimpsing of a better way of life, are not in themselves sufficient. To the " I know " must be added an " I will." Out of effective worship come moments of contrition, unrevealed confessions of error, determined resolution to measure up to the high level of human possibility.

Fifth, lasting life controls should be established. The whole religious education process has to do with habits, controls, directions of life. The worship experience is essential for most of us if habits are to be formed in opposition to those seemingly natural pulls toward evil, if any coördination between ideas and actions is to take place. An ultimate objective of worship, therefore, is so to fix the mind upon God, and to direct and give power to the will that impulses will be guided, desires be purged, habits of rectitude be established, and the whole man made responsive to the will of God.

Special Forms and Occasions of Worship

When a program of religious education becomes mechanized and completely regularized it is in danger of being dehumanized. We are constantly tempted to proceed in the same way, each Sunday, both in the division of time between instruction and worship and in our conduct of the worship itself. One of the chief causes of failure in church work can be found at just this point: sameness in procedure. It is, therefore, advisable that the church should not confine its worship features to the fifteen- or twenty-minute period preceding the class session and the five-minute closing service. It is equally necessary that there be variety in the content and conduct of these regular sessions. The following four suggestions merely hint at ways in which many leaders are supplementing the generally recognized usages and occasions.

1. Worship as the central feature of the hour. There are times when it is natural to worship, as there are other times when it is right to play and foolish to attempt any formal instruction. Some of these opportunities come suddenly, without any opportunity for detailed preparation; a skillful leader should recognize when such moments have arrived and should swing the group into a program of worship. There are other times when it can be predicted in advance that worship would be more fruitful than lectures or discussion. Such occasions are the Christmas season, when the reading of a great classic in story form induces an attitude of worship as natural and helpful as any educational process that could be devised; a vesper occasion in the late fall, when the group has hiked to a hilltop and the trees are gloriously outlined against the skies of twilight, and when nothing more natural than a service of song and the reading of nature poems could be desired; a communion service at the close of an institute, participated in by the young people of a parish or by the representatives from a variety of churches.

2. **The junior church.** Some of our larger churches have separated the young people from the adults for a service which parallels the so-called "preaching service." It may be held at the same hour as the general service in a room specially furnished for worship, or at an hour preceding or following the adult gathering. Where this plan of formal worship prevails, there is less need for a separate period of worship in connection with the instructional session of the church school, provided young people themselves share in the conduct of the worship in the junior church.

The order of worship is not much different from that of the church generally, except that the talk and the prayers and the other elements of worship are more specifically adapted to the intelligence and immediate needs of adolescents. In favor of this plan, it may be said that this is a natural way in which to enable young people to gain an appreciation and understanding of formal worship as represented in the morning worship of the church. It also offers opportunity for thoughtful participation in leadership in this extended worship hour.

Three cautions are suggested for those pastors and superintendents who contemplate the inauguration of this modern department of church life. The first is that the junior church program should be thought of as an integral part of the total religious education plan and not as something separate from it. The second fact which must be guarded is that those general principles upon which the religious education of adolescents is founded must apply also to this phase of the program; for instance, the age-groupings must be respected. The third is this: great care must be taken to make a natural transition from the junior church to the regular service of worship of the church after the young people have reached the senior age.

3. Ritualistic elements. Many young people are attracted by the ceremonials which form so large a feature in secret societies. Does this mean that the church should make more use of ritual? Or is it true that in the cities, at least, the young people are getting so much of this elsewhere that it would be unwise for church bodies to incorporate much of the ceremonial in their programs? Whatever the answer may be to this question of policy, it is certain that there are occasions when ritual has its place. In addition to the forms which are a part of the program of certain national organizations which work within the church, there should be some development of original ritual by the local group. For example, it is a good plan to have an impressive form to be followed in the welcoming of new members, a permanent service for the installation of officers, and an impressive commissioning ritual for delegates to summer conferences. Opening and closing services involving permanent ritualistic features are useful in some organizations, although for most groups it is probably wiser to reserve such forms for special occasions. Ritual can easily be overdone. It is much better to work hard on a few elements of ceremonial, to perfect them, and to make use of them once a month or so, than to make frequent use of poorly worked out ceremonials.

4. Symbolism in programs. In recent years, since ritualism has been making a new appeal to young and old, there has been a tendency in some quarters to look upon secret symbols as the great hope of young people's work, to take the view that ritualism in itself will assure numerical success in church work. But it is a mistake to substitute symbolism for genuine study and service. Whether young people are kept regular in attendance by an intelligent repetition of liturgies or not, it is not wise to think of rituals as a major element in a religious program. This loyalty to a form will not abide forever, and after the glow of its first joy has faded the leader will have all his original problems and responsibilities left. Just as going to church regularly and listening intently to a sermon is not in itself a guaranty of sincere and intelligent living, so interest in a ritualistic order does not provide a rounded religious education. It is important that every symbol used have genuine significance, and that the entire ceremonial be Christian in its foundation and its implications. Where elements of symbolic worth take their place as a part of a program, they are to be encouraged; but when a fraternity exalts the symbol and makes it a substitute for a program of study and work, it frustrates a complete program of Christian development and service.

Materials Recommended for Further Study

Councilor, Homer J. *The Junior Church.* Century.

Fosdick, Harry E. *The Meaning of Prayer.* Association Press.

Gates, O. Sherwood. *Youth and Worship.* International Council of Religious Education. (Christian Quest booklet.)

Harper, Earl E. *Church Music and Worship.* Abingdon Press.

Hartshorne, Hugh. *The Book of Worship of the Church School.* Scribner's.

——. *Manual for Training in Worship.* Scribner's.

Shaver, Erwin L. and Stock, Harry T. *Training Young People in Worship.* Pilgrim Press.

Sperry, Willard L. *Reality in Worship.* Macmillan.

Thurston, Mabel N. *The Adventure of Prayer.* Revell.

Vogt, Von Ogden. *Modern Worship.* Yale University Press.

Weigle, Luther A., and Tweedy, Henry H. *Training the Devotional Life.* Pilgrim Press.

Wieman, Henry N. *Methods of Private Religious Living.* Macmillan.

Worship Materials

The Abingdon Hymnal, edited by E. E. Harper. (Young people's edition.) Abingdon Press.

The American Student Hymnal, edited by H. A. Smith. Century.

The Church School Hymnal for Youth. Westminster Press.

Dramatic Activities for Young People, by Grace S. Overton. Century.

The Hymnal for American Youth, edited by H. A. Smith. Century.

The Hymnal for Young People, edited by M. S. Littlefield and Margaret Slattery. Barnes.

Readings from Great Authors, edited by J. H. Holmes and others. Dodd, Mead.

Services for the Open, edited by Laura I. Mattoon and Helen D. Bragdon. Century.

Song and Worship for Young People, edited by S. A. Weston. Pilgrim Press.

Dramatic Services of Worship, by Isabel K. Whiting. Beacon Press.

Worship and Song, edited by B. S. Winchester and G. W. Conant. Pilgrim Press.

Worship for Youth, by Gussie B. Stacy. Powell and White.

The Book of Common Prayer. Morehouse.

A Book of Prayers for Students. London, Student Christian Movement.

The Girl's Every Day Book. Womans Press.

Poems of Action. David R. Porter. Association Press.

Prayers of the Social Awakening. Walter Rauschenbusch. Pilgrim Press.

Young Men and Prayer. Thomas R. Richards. Pilgrim Press.

A Girl's Book of Prayer. Margaret Slattery. Pilgrim Press.

CHAPTER VII

THE OUTREACH OF SERVICE

"I DON'T see why we should be expected to carry out a program of service. We have good meetings, discuss the things that we're interested in, are loyal to the church, and get a lot out of our organization. Why should we always be asked to do something for somebody else?" This was the good-spirited comment of an intelligent young man in one of the larger churches of the Mississippi Valley.

There is on the part of many program promoters a pronounced insistence that we always be "doing somebody else good." Our age needs to be brought back from its noisy hereness-and-thereness. It has become a habit to argue that no program is worth much unless it can show a prominent section labeled "service activities." That impatience which chafes at the idea that in order to be religious a man must be eternally busy saving some one or reforming him or serving him is thoroughly justified. That idea of religious education which measures the worth of activities in terms of results which can be seen, weighed, tested, or tabulated fails to take account of the deep inner qualities of religion or the far-off results of education. It would be better for many groups if they were less actively engaged in devious perfunctory committee tasks and were more thoughtfully employed in serious study and meaningful worship.

Still the young man's plea was not justified. His viewpoint extended to the logical conclusion would make of the church a receptive smug institution, more concerned with its own health and comfort than it is with the sin and sorrow and need of the social order. The young people who were present at this evening meeting came from homes of considerable wealth. The community is full of all types of human problems; the outreach of organized good-will through this church is practically unlimited in its possibility. The denomination of which the church is a part is engaged in large enterprises, reaching all around the world, attempting to carry out the intention of Christ in ways wholly consistent with that gospel and with modern science and pedagogy.

Here were young people, loyal to the church to the extent of spending Sunday night there instead of in the theaters or in automobiles, eager to listen to intelligent leaders. They were being builded up in a knowledge of life, they thought, and thus they were doing enough for Christianity. The many demands which pressed upon this church were not apparent to them. They were wholly impervious to the idea that they had responsibility for the hunger and sorrow and sin of that neighborhood. One cannot blame them for being weary of appeals in the name of "service," but they are not blameless if they continue blind to their responsibility for those unfortunate neighbors. Their leadership is not guiltless if during the years that they are growing into manhood and womanhood they are not introduced to a sense of responsibility for mankind everywhere, a responsibility which is not only theoretical but which is inescapable in its demands for immediate participation. It is not for the sake of an abstract "service" that young people are urged to be active. It is in the interests of humanity that they are summoned to sacrificial living.

The Place of Service in the Program

1. Service as a part of a project. In the discussion of the curriculum attention was called to the importance of the project principle. Emphasis was placed upon the fact that a curriculum conceived in functional terms will often involve the young people in undertakings which demand considerable physical activity. This is a part of the natural process, just as much a part of it as the studying of books or quarterlies or the discussion of the class. Service is often the starting point for discussion and study: a good deed done to some one in need may be the means of bringing into perspective the whole obligation of the church with reference to community philanthropies. Service may also be an outcome of a project: a group that has completed a study of the religions of non-Christian lands may be so convinced of the need of Christian missions that it eagerly initiates a plan by which it may assume responsibility for some particular foreign object; or service may be a part of the project, at some point in the study, being both an outcome of expressed interest and the basis for further research.

2. **Regular service duties assumed by the young people's group.** There are many week-by-week activities of the church, not directly connected with the subjects for class study, which may be carried on by the young people themselves. Such regular duties establish a sense of ownership in the church on the part of the young people, and make it certain that the subsidiary organizations have an increasing understanding that their life is tied up in the being of the church itself. Thousands of adults owe their present allegiance to the organized work of Christianity to the fact that when they were in classes or societies they shared such tasks as the following: distributing the flowers at the close of the church service among families where there was sickness, collecting books and magazines for distribution among the sick of the parish, calling in automobiles for the aged in order that they might share the benefits of Sunday church attendance. These may seem to be trivial activities; they are not much different from the chores which boys and girls of a previous generation were obliged to do. But they are an expression of the will to serve, they are means of aiding the character-formation

process, they are also genuine contributions to social happiness. It is especially important that regular duties of this type shall be offered to those of the intermediate age.

Other more "important tasks" (viewed from the standpoint of the older young people) are the following: serving as junior deacons, sharing in the choir activities, acting as regular ushers along with older members of the church, responsibility for primary or junior groups of boys and girls, being full-fledged members of important committees of the church, planning and carrying out the remodeling of the young people's room in the building, accepting a specific phase of responsibility for missionary or community campaigns.

3. "Unto all the nations, beginning from Jerusalem." The honest skepticism of the young man who was unconvinced of the necessity of service as a part of a program is matched by two other viewpoints which show themselves in common practice. First, we have the readiness of earnest Christians to try to ameliorate the unfortunate conditions within a local community, a conviction that the church must evangelize and serve those within its local parish, but an equally sure unwillingness to join in any effort to improve conditions in adjacent communities or to extend the arm of helpfulness across the seas. Second, there is a common interest among adults and young people in the far-away, which frequently blinds them to the grimy duties for which they are responsible in the near-at-hand areas.

Few of our groups are able to do a great deal to improve life either in the immediate vicinity or in foreign lands. The needs are so great and the abilities of small groups so limited that it seems almost hopeless to try to do anything. Why, it may be asked, would it not be better to center all effort upon a single enterprise, in the hope of sharpening the interest of the group and of making some appreciable gain at a single point? This is, indeed, in line with the whole project emphasis: to concentrate the thought and activity of a group upon a specific interest, rather than to study missions in general or to support financially a program of service handed down by a board. One of the most hopeful developments in the service programs of our classes and societies is just here: they know whom they want to help, they understand just what help is needed, they have some kind of personal contact with the workers who are employed in the missionary program, and their study and work center upon the opportunities in this selected field. There is danger, of course, that a group may become so thoroughly and permanently related to this single enterprise that they will not see its relation to the whole range of human need and service. The leader must take care that participation in this definite piece of work leads to an understanding of world-wide need, to an eagerness to know about and at least to sympathize with the efforts that are everywhere being made to develop a civilization based upon brotherhood, to secure a constructive and critical and warm-hearted loyalty to the idea for which the words "missions" and "service" should stand.

World service, world friendship, missions — these are not localized terms. The service program of the church should be an attempt of organized Christians to play the part of the disciple efficiently, to act the part of the neighbor to all the children of men. In this effort we seek to avoid a bothersome interference with the business of others, to save ourselves from all superciliousness and from the notion that we are wholly competent to purvey to misguided pagans a superior goodness which we possess in abundance. Because we live in a community we share its sins and virtues and common tasks. Because we are a part of a small world our obligations extend to the farther reaches of the globe.

4. Money as service. The giving of money is our most common means of service. The obligations of young people in this regard must be carefully studied if the process of religious education is to produce its full fruitage. A plan of systematic, proportional and sacrificial giving should issue from any such study. But one of the sins of the adult world is its reliance upon the giving of money as its sole means of service. This method of vicarious service will always be necessary; as our society grows more complicated and our means of aiding humanity more scientific, our reliance upon experts will increase. It is, therefore, a part of the task of the church school to create a growing interest in those who are skillfully ministering to human wants, and to match this interest with a devoted practice of benevolent giving.

But Christian service must never be the actual practice of only a few, while Christian giving takes the place of first-hand ministry for the many. Competent adults cannot excuse themselves from teaching a class of boys simply by giving a few dollars to employ a "professional worker" who is unable to communicate that influence and character which these particular representatives of community life alone could pass on. Prominent leaders in business affairs do not fulfill their complete duty when they write a check which makes possible something more than a bare existence for a poor family. Young people will not develop the right conception of Christian duty if they are led to believe that the giving of quarters or dollars is the outstanding form of Christian service today. There are people who need friendliness more than they need Christmas trees, who need to be made to feel that they belong to the community even more than they need the cast-off clothing which a charitable institution can provide. And a part of the whole plan of ministry is that those who seek to serve in the name of Christ find that their contacts with the "unfortunates" usually bring into their own lives as rich a contribution as that which they seek to communicate. Perhaps, what is needed is that the words "neighborliness" or "friendliness" should be substituted for "missions" and "service." Thus our attitude of superiority might eventually pass, and in its place would come the thought of living with people for the sake of all; of being ready to give gladly of what we have, expecting at the same time to receive as much in this experience of common friendship as we can possibly give.

Intelligent Sharing in Missions

No single church could have an efficient wide outreach by itself. Within its community it can render a service fundamental and distinctive, but without denominational and interdenominational coöperation in world-wide service, Christianity would be impotent to meet the obligations of the present hour. Most local churches have, therefore, recognized the importance of acting with their sister organizations in making possible the plans which national leaders have initiated, both in the home and the foreign fields. While there has been too much blind acceptance of these programs on the one hand and too much dodging of all responsibility on the other, it is generally agreed that missionary boards must act as the authorized agents of the churches throughout the world. It is the duty of the churches to see that denominational boards administer funds wisely, and conduct missions on a basis both intelligent and prophetically Christian. It is their duty also to look upon the work projected by these authorized boards as the specific responsibility of the total Christian membership: the plans agreed upon are not to be resented by local leaders as enforced burdens. They ought not to be automatically accepted without discriminating study, but they should be taken with such modifications as the ability and resource of the local group demand. When a church has agreed to join in this general service project, it is usually well for the various departments of the church to take their fair share of the whole.

Because the range of activities covered under the head of " missions " is so wide, it is true for most churches that a large part of the actual service outside of its organized parish is carried on as a part of its "missionary program." The same is true of the young people's organizations. Because service must be based upon intelligence, and because missionary education is an essential prerequisite of wise world-service, it is important here to indicate certain possible phases of the program of education which must accompany the service activities of the school and society.

1. A study of the sanctions for the missionary enterprise. The older generation has had a feeble enthusiasm for missions; the younger generation will not develop a deeper loyalty unless it understands the what and why of missions. If the church enables them to come to an appreciation of the reasons for world service and of the values which are being produced by the missionary program, it will not only render the Kingdom of God a wide service, but it will contribute to the development of a sane and unselfish attitude on the part of the young people themselves.

The first basic consideration, therefore, in the curricular study of missions is that of acquainting adolescents with the continuing loyalty of Christian disciples to the great commission of Jesus. It will cover such a series of considerations as the following: Jesus' ministry was that of a missionary — a life of devotion and service to others; his disciples were trained that they might carry on this work when he laid down his life; the existence of Christianity in the world today is due to the fidelity with which these disciples continued this ministry and to the sacrificial support of the mass of early church members; from a small sect in Palestine, Christianity extended its influence throughout the whole Roman Empire; wherever civilization spread during the Middle Ages, missionaries carried the cross of Christ; when America was being settled, missionaries from Europe brought organized religion to our shores and wove Christianity into the very fabric of our national life; with the first settlers who crossed the Hudson and went from the south into the new west went missionaries from the churches in the east; in the early nineteenth century, American Christians began to feel their responsibility for missions in non-Christian lands, and the foreign missionary movement from America began; the present missionary program within America and beyond its confines is the fruitage and the continuation of the missionary zeal which was in Jesus and which during each generation was transmitted to devoted disciples. The history of Christianity has been the history of missions. The growth of the church has been the expression of the missionary spirit. The permeation of society by Christian ideas and ideals, slow as it is, has been the fruitage of Christian ministry. Most of the churches in America are either directly or indirectly the results of missionary labors.

2. **A study of the needs of the world today.** There is a grave question in the minds of many young people as to whether it is necessary to export Christianity to lands where Mohammedanism is proving satisfactory to the natives, and whether in a day when the American frontier has passed it is worth while to carry on the program of extension within our land. It will not do to answer them with a categorical assurance that they are wrong; indeed, they may not be entirely wrong. But they cannot be right, so long as they simply have " feelings " or prejudices instead of reasoned conclusions which grow out of knowledge. Nothing would do the church more good than to engage in a serious study of world needs; and if from that study should emerge the conclusion that much of the missionary program is unnecessary, it would be a revelation which every honest leader should desire to have made. But if it became manifest that the world is still sick, that humanity is in dire need of the Great Physician, that social disorder and international discord can be overcome only as the healing and binding power of Christianity is transmitted to the people of all nations, that the world wants still the Pauline power and daring which will lead to the accusation that modern Christians

have "turned the world upside down" — certainly the younger generation of Christians could be depended upon to give of their lives and resources that the dreams of the prophets might be brought to pass.

3. **A study of the program of modern missions.** When young people are asked to describe the picture in their minds when the word "missions" is mentioned, they reveal a paucity of information regarding the essential characteristics of this world-wide enterprise. There are two ways in which young people may be helped to visualize the field of Christian world service. One is to assist them in the study of some particular field of labor; the other is to begin with the total outreach of the church. In either case, there should be such wealth of detail that the "big business" character of missions is understood, and that the human aspects of the missionary's task are appreciated.

In discovering what types of missionaries are employed, what kinds of institutions are erected, what activities fill the days, what types of human need are constantly met, what results are sought and secured, all the various methods of religious education may be employed: there will be the listing and cataloguing of facts; pictures and articles will be clipped and placed conspicuously on a bulletin board; local situations will be dramatized for worship or study periods; letters may be written; clothes will be made or collected. All the thrill which comes from sharing in a project will almost certainly be assured to those who begin to appraise the present-day missionary outreach. Earnest-minded youth can hardly refrain from generous sharing after they have once envisioned the world's need and the church's opportunity for meeting it.

And in such a study there should be included the whole question of interdenominational coöperation. Young people are particularly susceptible to the well-meant and much-needed criticisms of church-unionists, who decry the divisions at home and abroad and try to shame the administrators of missionary enterprises by pointing out the wastes and sins of denominationalism. It is right to fan the eager enthusiasm of young people into revolt against sectarianism; they must lead in bringing unity to the cause of Christ. But the danger is that in their eagerness to rid the missionary enterprise of narrowness they may overlook the degree of coöperation which now exists and may injure the effectiveness of the good work now in progress. It is important, therefore, that the survey of the present program of missions shall take into account interdenominational coöperation in planning, administering, and conducting the work of mission fields. This should come into the purview of young people not with the intention of justifying denominationalism, but with the purpose of enabling them to see the whole picture.

4. A frank study of the obligation of the local church. Who is responsible for the boards of the denominations? How are they selected? Who gives them authority for their programs? Where do they secure their resources? What is the relation of your church to them? Has your church ever received any money from any of the benevolent boards? Does it to any degree owe its life to the organized activities of the denomination? To what extent does the on-going program of the denomination depend upon your church?

It will be discovered that organized Christianity cannot function successfully without the coöperation of all of its local units. Several methods of apportioning the responsibility prevail. One of them is that each church is asked to contribute such a sum as it can pay to the total program of the boards. Another is that each local unit is asked to adopt some specific field or activity as its own responsibility. Either plan is intended to secure the united effort of the denomination behind the total work of the church. In either case, the membership should be informed regarding the large outlines of the denominational program and concerning the detailed methods in some specific field. It would seem that these methods are "handed down" schemes for participation in service. "Who gives the board the right to ask us for a certain amount?" is the question which formulates itself in the minds of many thoughtful young people. The answer should be discovered in the study which has been suggested in the preceding section: the boards are the creations of the churches, are controlled by them, are attempting to carry on the extension program of these churches, and must necessarily be supported by them. The askings of the boards should, therefore, be subjected to thoughtful consideration by the local units and the decisions should be made in the light of needs and resources. Usually it is wise for the church-school classes or departments or for the society to assume a share of the total acceptance of the local church.

5. A plan of study related to the objects which the local group has chosen. Suppose it is decided that the young people's group of a given church will undertake two pieces of work: assistance to an Indian school in the West, and the maintenance of a hospital bed in China. Throughout the year, the responsible committee should see to it that fresh information comes regarding the use which is being made of the funds sent. In addition, it will probably be the desire of the young people to make bedding and bandages, or to provide clothing for the persons whom they are trying to befriend. The bulletin board will be used to give publicity to new information. Letters will be read from those who have received the gifts. Dramatizations will be introduced as features in the worship or study periods. Perhaps an entire quarter will be given to a project centering around Indian missions or medical service abroad.

6. A study of missionary textbooks. The Missionary Education Movement publishes books which are recommended by most of the denominations as being well adapted to the various age groups. These books, or others of an equally high character, may be inserted into the regular study curriculum of the church-school classes, covering an entire quarter or serving as part of a quarter's program; or special groups may be interested in spending an extra session a week, for a month or two, in the study of one of these volumes; or there may be reviews of the successive chapters by different young people as a part of the class or departmental program at given periods in the year. In "church schools of missions," conducted either in the late autumn or during the Lenten period, there may be classes for all age groups, during which time some of these volumes are covered.

7. Missions in the Sunday evening meetings. The common procedure for young people's societies has been to have a missionary topic once a month. These topics have usually been very general in character; the helps have given little real information upon the subjects under discussion; the meetings have been poorly prepared for and consequently have been productive of as much dislike for missions as of loyalty to the cause. Dry missionary meetings are worse than none. In order to make such sessions interesting and useful it is necessary to have topics which are specific and significant, a committee which makes faithful preparation for the meetings, great variety in the conduct of the program. All the methods which have been discussed elsewhere in this volume — reading books together, dramatizations, forums led by competent visitors — may be employed in the missionary program of the society.

There are those who believe that the topic-a-month idea is the best one, because it keeps the emphasis coming throughout the entire year and does not run the danger of having "too much missions" all at once. The difficulty with the plan is that it makes for haphazardness in program. There is comparatively little carry-over from one month to the next. The meetings are likely to be more or less interesting sessions in themselves without issuing in working plans which find their consummation during a series of weeks of work. Wherever it is possible, therefore, it is recommended that a series of related missionary themes be formulated, to cover four to six weeks of study and activity, and that one such series be incorporated into the fall program and another into the spring schedule, on consecutive Sundays.

Service as Opportunity

The whole procedure of the leadership should be such that young people will not think of service as a duty which they must needs fulfill in order to be loyal members. There is something more fundamental than either duty or loyalty. Jesus ministered to mankind not primarily because he felt it to be his duty; he did it out of love — love for mankind in the concrete as well as in the abstract, and love for God. This love for God and for man involved a loyalty — a loyalty which grew out of affection. And it is that affection which we need above all to help to establish. Once young people have a compelling love for God and a consuming love for people, service will be the natural expression of the inner experience. It will not be thought of in terms of duty, but of opportunity and privilege. It will not so much be a fulfilment of loyalty to an institution as an expression of the Christianity that moves within a life.

Materials Recommended for Further Study

Cope, Henry F. *Principles of Christian Service.* Judson Press.
Fleming, Daniel J. *Marks of a World Christian.* Association Press.
Fosdick, Harry E. *The Meaning of Service.* Association Press.
Gates, Herbert W. *Missionary Education in the Church.* Pilgrim Press.
Hutchins, Norman W. *Graded Social Service in the Sunday School.* University of Chicago Press.

Lobingier, John L. *Projects in World Friendship.* University of Chicago Press.

——. *World Friendship through the Church School.* University of Chicago Press.

——. *Youth and the World Outlook.* Pilgrim Press.

McFadyen, Joseph F. *The Missionary Idea in Life and Religion.* Scribner's.

Speer, Robert E. *The Church and Missions.* Revell.

Missionary Education in the Local Church. Congregational Education Society.

Chapter VIII

THE FINANCIAL PROGRAM

"THE love of money is a root of all kinds of evil," and carelessness in the use of money is an outstanding sin of young and old. It is true of families; it is equally true of churches. The church universal is charged with holding a materialistic viewpoint because it talks too much in terms of statistics and measures its importance by the millions of dollars of invested funds and the enormous annual outlay for current expenses. On the other hand, trustees and treasurers permit methods in the raising and expenditure of monies which they would not tolerate in any business over which they exercised control and in which they had a stockholder's stake. Almost never are young people given wise counsel regarding the financial program of their own department or societies. Haphazard methods of securing funds are used by the young people. The most unbusinesslike forms of bookkeeping are condoned. Expenditures are on the basis of emotional slants rather than on that of sound reason.

Young people need to be led to contribute regularly and sacrificially to the program of the church and of its subsidiary agencies for two main reasons:

1. The Church needs the support of the young people. From the days of the first Christians until now the giving of money has been considered one of the tests of Christian devotion. In a world in which no enterprise can be carried on without funds, the church has a right to expect hearty and unstinted giving on the part of all its friends. This applies no less to young people than it does to their elders, for young people have money to divide.

First, the local program of the church must be maintained. Is the church a city set on a hill, or is it a weak voice crying unheard in some neglected corner of the neighborhood? Does it compare in attractiveness of setting and equipment with the commercial allurements on the main street? Do those who feel that they " own " the church cherish it, through their gifts, to the same degree that they contribute to the bank accounts of the theater owners?

Second, the local church has a responsibility beyond its parish. At no time in Christian history has a local group been excused from the necessity of " making disciples of all men," of bringing abundance of life to the farther reaches of the earth. A non-missionary church is a non-Christian church. A non-social church is a non-Christian church.

Third, the church must not " always be asking for money." Young people complain that almost every conference or institute is climaxed by an appeal for funds. They resent the fact that at many times during the year their organizations are urged to support causes about which they know little. Just as many adults stay away from the morning service when the traditional " missionary sermon " is preached, so young people resist the idea that they are good material for the financial exploitation of adult enthusiasts. The church should not " always " be asking for money. But it should have no hesitation in urging young and old to maintain those causes which are legitimately its responsibility. It should make its case definite and should concentrate its appeals.

2. **The young people need the religious and educational values which come from personal giving and from group endeavor.** It is difficult enough for this generation to grow up with right ideas of success, with a proper sense of values.

Mealtime conversation at home is full of financial perplexity and discussion. The adult world is a round of competitive effort not only to " keep up with the Joneses " but to get ahead of them. The social life of high schools and colleges is on a level of extravagance which develops tastes and habits far from that modest and reasonable level which sanity would dictate. Allowances are never large enough, no matter how generous they are. The tendency is completely away from all self-denial. There is resentment at all efforts to limit pleasure and expenditure by any form of social control, such as might be exercised through family agreements. A most common cause of disagreements between parents and children (as between husbands and wives) is the money problem. The idea of the " simple life " has gone from present-day society. One of the pressing duties of Christian agencies is to bring back perspective, to emphasize the idea of life as a ministry instead of a perpetual effort for personal satiety, to make the belief in the necessity of being our brother's keeper something more than a glibly recited ideal, to provide a real taste of the joy that comes from self-denial in the interests of a worthy cause.

First, leaders must recognize that two of the ever-present and universal problems of youth are those of the division of time and money. If we build a curriculum which has the " hot spots " of current life as a central element, no class or society program should ignore these specific temptations which young people face daily. Service and giving and missionary endeavor belong inside the curriculum, without apology.

Second, young people should be led to a full realization that future happiness and usefulness are being determined by present habits. Honest or crooked business men are being made during high-school days. Economical or extravagant householders are being grown now. Tight-fisted or philanthropic church leaders will graduate from the young people's division. If there is any justification for our belief in the superior value of religious education over the evangelistic process, it is that we shall actually grow a more Christian generation of adults. Time alone will tell whether our faith in our present methods is well grounded; but we do not need to wait for the fruition of decades to know that if young people in our church schools now do not begin during adolescent days to deny themselves luxuries or necessities for the sake of a world brotherhood, nothing but a genuine adult conversion will ever bring it about.

Third, young people need to develop a Christian philosophy of life which puts getting and saving and giving and spending in their proper perspective. Modern life is moved by impulse and not by loyalty to reasoned convictions. As Benjamin Franklin said, " So convenient a thing it is to be a reasonable creature, since it enables one to find or make a reason for anything one has a mind to do." That was not the method of Jesus, and it is not the one which will ever establish the Kingdom of God. The churches have been placing a new emphasis upon stewardship. The modern proponents of this idea have made the term a very inclusive one. As its champions define it, it is nothing less than living the Christian life: it is being a Christian. If that is what stewardship is, we would do better to stop talking about stewardship and begin to place the emphasis upon being Christians. " Stewardship," at any rate, is not a good word to use with young people. It has no relationship to the social life with which they are acquainted; it is an adult term out of touch with the phraseology of the century. It is better to talk plainly with young people about the " Christian's use of money." Any real consideration of financial obligations should begin with or end with or involve the formulation of a set of principles which seem to the young people to express the Christian's duty in money matters. This controlling philosophy will not be developed by a lecture, an hour's discussion, or a financial appeal.

A Single Budget for the Entire Church?

Some churches have adopted the plan whereby there is a single treasury, one budget, and a unified financial program for all of the agencies connected with the church. The theory behind this plan runs as follows: The church is the central institution to which the loyalty of old and young should be stimulated; it is the one agency responsible for the local and world-wide program of religion, and all monies used in this program should be contributed directly to it and should be expended as it determines; all of the subsidiary organizations have reason for their existence primarily because of their relation to the church and they should have no programs not integral with that of the central body.

From the practical standpoint there has been good ground for the development of this completely unified plan. Some young people attend church services three or four times a week; at all of these meetings offerings are taken. The result is that some of them are embarrassed at the frequency with which they are expected to contribute; and when it is possible to give something each time, the amount given to any agency is not likely to be large. There are a number of small budgets. The work of the several agencies is not correlated and is sometimes sadly inconsistent. The young people have learned the habit of giving small sums to religious causes. Perhaps the last organization to be remembered in any systematic way is the church itself. The young people have given to the class, the society, the missionary guild, and they may or may not drop a nickel into the collection at the Sunday morning church service. Rarely do they pledge a definite sum of any considerable size to the annual program of the church itself.

In the unified plan, the budget committee of the church would make out its program of askings and undertakings for adoption before the beginning of a year. Each agency of the church would also make out its schedule of money needed for its local enterprises and its list of projects which should be supported by the church. The church committee would then consider the reports of these subsidiary bodies. It would include in its total budget such of the projects of the church school, the young people's society and other agencies as it thought deserved support. It would, moreover, appropriate a monthly sum for the maintenance of the school and society, and the treasurers of these agencies would receive their monies from the church treasury. No collections would be taken in the society or department meetings, except that envelopes which might be turned in at these gatherings would go directly to the church treasurer. Each young person would, therefore, feel under the necessity of contributing but once a week and his contribution might, consequently, be large enough to give him a real pride in having aided the work of the church significantly.

There are arguments against this plan which deserve consideration. The first is that young people will not give so much money under such a scheme as under the common plan of contributing even a small sum to each agency. They will not pledge, say, twenty dollars a year to the church. One answer is that by a process of education they might be brought to the point of making the larger pledge, provided they had a genuine enthusiasm for the church and this unified plan. The fact that they give more generously without planning or real intelligence, should not elate us. Unless they learn to give regularly, proportionally, and intelligently, their contributions will not increase as their income grows, and they will not hold the church treasury in the high regard which it deserves when the church is functioning effectively.

A much more important objection to this plan is that it relieves the young people's organization of most of the responsibility for the handling and control of its own money. Final authority rests with the church — the adult part of the church. Business transactions are taken care of *for* the young people instead of *by* them, except for that small sum which comes from the church treasurer for incidental purposes. It may be questioned whether such an arrangement is either fair or educational.

It is a common experience of pastors and young people and women's organizations that " the church treasurer is the tightest person in the church "; " the board of trustees seem to think that their main business is to cut down expenses and hoard money." The main concern of some is that the boys and girls do not break up the furniture; they may use the church building provided they give assurance that the chairs will remain intact. Is there any likelihood that under this unified scheme, the adult board or committee would think that the service objectives of the society deserved support, that even such an item as fifteen dollars for a church-school library would be approved? Is it not the business of the church school and the society to support the church (they would argue), and not the business of the church to provide non-necessities for the school and society? It might be countered: Is it the business of the adolescent to support his father and mother? Shall the desires, the philanthropic ambitions of boys and girls, all be held up for approval or veto by the parent, and shall they have no freedom in the choice of their good enterprises?

If any church plans to adopt this unified arrangement (which, from the standpoint of fundamental theory seems right because it places the church in the central position that it deserves, provides an opportunity for unity of action and a minimum of waste, and seeks to encourage young people to include a sizable sum for religion in their personal budgets), it should see to it that the budget committee is not " stacked " against the young people or against any organization of the church. If men and women who have no religious educational vision and who are concerned only with getting as much and spending as little as possible dominate the committee, the results will surely be disastrous. Certainly, every agency concerned should be represented on this church committee: the church school, the societies, the women's organizations.

The Necessity for a Budget

Whether the money is to pass through the church treasury or that of the young people's organization, there should be an annual budget carefully made out, discussed, adopted, and adhered to. At the beginning of the year, such questions as the following should be raised: How much did we spend last year? How great are the needs for the coming year? How much should this group of young people be able to give? What is the minimum that we shall agree to raise? The budget committee should weigh the importance of the various objects in which the members are interested and should recommend that the division of the money be upon a percentage basis; for example, the following sample (agreed upon by a group of summer conference delegates) may be used as the point of departure:

Running expenses	20%
Local church program	25%
Church missionary program	25%
Miscellaneous service projects	15%
Miscellaneous and emergencies	15%

Under each of such headings, certain specific causes may be named. It may be that the young people will want to make a definite contribution to the pastor's salary or to the music for the church services. They may want to help support a particular missionary field or to contribute directly to the national young people's program of the denomination. One of their miscellaneous service projects may be the support of the State Council of Religious Education, the Christian Endeavor Union, or some similar fellowship. The important point is that all such projects should be included in the budget. The young people should not be stampeded at various periods of the year into giving handsome sums for outside causes, whether worthy or not. These may, of course, be considered, but if they are to be supported the money should usually come from the "emergency" item unless the majority wish to take a special offering.

Just how seriously should a budget be taken? Should it be just a general guide? Should we be irrevocably bound by it? The following principles represent a reasonable attitude:

1. A budget is the best possible forecast of the minimum that the group will raise during the year.

2. The individual items contained in it should be met before any additional burden is assumed, unless something of real significance has been omitted or some sudden emergency arises which clearly challenges the interest of the entire group.

3. The budget can be amended only by vote of the body.

4. The budget should be large enough to make the group work hard the whole year to measure up to its demands. It does not restrict the maximum amount which may be raised.

5. It is often a good plan to have two budgets: a minimum budget and a desirable budget. The minimum schedule would represent that sum below which the receipts must not fall; the desirable budget represents the higher total toward which the group will strive.

What Should Be Included in a Budget?

No one can make a budget to order for young people's departments or societies in general. Every local group must make its own. Denominational headquarters should not try to determine the giving of society or class, in detail or by paternalistic methods. They may make suggestions but when these suggestions are given in a tone of authority they arouse the suspicion that they intend the exploitation of youth in the interests of an adult program. Even the local church should not try to legislate the details of a young people's budget. There are, however, certain causes which universally and logically appeal to young people and are usually included in their schedules. The following are some of them.

1. **The group program.** How much does the department need for speakers, music, the week-to-week costs? What per cent of the total is required? Not a very large portion, perhaps, unless the program provides for a considerable number of speakers whose expenses must be met.

2. **The church program.** The society or department is a part of the church. It will want to share part of the general program of the larger body.

3. **The missionary or extension program.** Many young people desire to have a conspicuous share in the missionary or benevolent program of their church or of the community, provided the needs are truly apparent and the money which they give is assured of accomplishing a desired end.

4. **Other service objectives.** There are certain local charities which will need help. There will sometimes be a difference of opinion as to whether young people should contribute directly to the recognized " charity organizations," or whether they should seek out persons who are not aided by these bodies. Two general considerations may be kept in mind: (a) most of these philanthropic agencies have workers well equipped to understand the needs of unfortunate families and their judgment can usually be relied upon, whereas those of us who are untrained in social investigation frequently feel a sympathy which is not well placed and consequently do as much harm as good; (b) whatever is done by young people should be of such a character that some personal relationship is established with those helped, a relationship which will prove useful to both the helpers and the helped.

5. Interdenominational fellowships. There should be an item covering miscellaneous demands or emergency needs. Within this classification might be included such causes as the State Council of Religious Education, the Christian Endeavor Union, etc. In considering the amount to be given to such bodies, a comparison should be made with the amount suggested for the local church and the denominational missionary program. The sums given to each should be based partly upon the degree of service rendered by each, and in every case it should be decided calmly by the committee in the light of need and program. No such decisions should be determined by delegates when they are away at conventions. This, along with all other items, should be taken up in the budget sessions before the beginning of the year. If this has not been done, delegates may make recommendations when they return from conferences but they should not make pledges at these gatherings unless specifically authorized to do so before leaving home, and such authorization should be for a definite amount. It has been agreed by the secretaries of the Christian Endeavor movement and by most of the denominational young people's secretaries that fifteen per cent of the total budget constitutes a fair amount for the various union activities.

Methods of Raising Funds

Several methods of raising money are in use among young people's groups.

1. Dues. In the church-school classes the policy of fixed dues seldom prevails, but it is a common practice in young people's societies and clubs. The advantage of this scheme is that it sets a minimum expectation around which a budget can be confidently built, and it secures a regularity of contribution. The arguments against it are that the sum fixed as a monthly due is likely to be so small that it does not train in sacrificial giving, nor will the receipts make possible a large enough budget. Moreover, it puts everyone on the same basis — well-to-do and poor, those who are earning money and those who receive small allowances.

2. **Collections.** Many who do not like the idea of fixed dues prefer the method of voluntary offerings, taken either every week or every month. While this allows greater personal freedom, it is likely to produce a small income unless the young people study conscientiously their responsibility for Christian enterprises and faithfully act upon the conclusions reached. They will probably put into the offering the smallest coin that they have; even so it may average ten cents a person. But those who do not attend on a given week will not feel obliged to send an offering, as ought to be the case where the dues system prevails. Consequently, it is not possible to figure as definitely in advance what the year's income is likely to be, and the budget will need to be more flexible.

3. **Pledges.** The church plans to secure the major portion of its income from pledges made by members and friends. In some church schools, the same plan is in effect; that is to say, every child and young person and adult is asked to make a weekly pledge to the church school or class, whether it be one cent or twenty-five. This is an effective money-raiser, especially among the lower grades, for parents are likely to encourage the giving of a nickel whereas on the voluntary collection basis they might send only a penny.

There is no reason why this plan will not work equally well in the society or club. It may be questioned whether the amount given will be much larger than if the fixed due system prevailed, but it avoids the possible embarrassment which might come to some of the less affluent members and it will lead the more conscientious to give a larger sum than they might otherwise contribute. There is a psychological objection which will make this scheme unwelcome in some places: where there are already several organizations being run on the pledge system, the members will resent the thought of an additional pledge, although they may be willing to contribute without signing a card.

4. **A combination of two of these plans.** As a general principle it is not wise to have a fixed due and a regular weekly collection, especially if the young people are expected to contribute to other organizations on the same day; but it may be understood that at certain times, special offerings will be taken for specific objects. There may be a monthly offering for missions, or there may be opportunities for giving in connection with specific enterprises which are discussed at the regular meetings of the class and society, periodically throughout the year.

5. **Letting the other person pay the bills.** Most young people's groups plan to raise a large part of their money from outside sources, through socials and entertainments. This is a method which relieves them individually of major financial responsibility for the program, except as they must contribute work and materials. As long as they give value received for the entrance fee no serious charge can be brought against "pay socials." One of the finest results is not financial: it is that a group of young people have worked hard on some large task and have learned some of the lessons of coöperation and responsibility which can become their possession only through such experience. But there are certain cautions which must be observed if these entertainments are to make constructive contributions to the religious and educational life of the group.

First, main dependence should not be placed upon this means of raising money. It ought to be considered only as a means of supplementing the regular, proportional giving of the young people.

Second, it must be remembered that very often this is an uneconomical method of raising money. More time and effort and money are spent in getting ready to raise income through socials than the results justify. Parents would save money if they increased their giving directly instead of giving the added sum in eggs and butter for the baking of cakes.

Third, any commercial undertaking under the auspices of the church should give full value for money received. In fact, it should give a little more than full value. The common joke about the one oyster in a plate of soup indicates the reputation that the church has in this regard. In selling ice cream, a church should give a dish at least as large as that which may be purchased for the same price at a confectioner's. The same principle should be observed in the matter of entertainment, and it should scarcely need to be added that there must not be a single suggestion of coarseness in any number of the program.

Fourth, church people should not take advantage of good-natured business men. They are often willing to secure materials for the church at cost price, they permit posters to be placed in their store windows, they lend various properties and utensils (which are not always returned in perfect condition). These may be legitimate requests to make of them, but care should be taken when it comes to soliciting advertising for programs. It is often true that the so-called advertising which merchants are asked to insert in programs for concerts and plays does not result in a single cent of increased business for them. It cannot be properly charged to advertising; it is clearly a gift to the church. When half a dozen churches in a community solicit such gifts under the guise of advertising, the merchants may submit gracefully, but almost always they bear an inner resentment which is usually justified. They sometimes charge the church with getting this money under false pretenses, and yet they dare not say so aloud. It would be much better if printed programs could be dispensed with, unless the cost is borne by merchants who themselves express voluntarily a willingness to contribute to the church in this way. This whole question is one of many which a young people's group might well discuss some Sunday evening as a problem in business ethics. In its discussion the judgment of local business men might be secured, not only that of genuine friends of the church but of merchants who are apathetic to religious institutions.

Collecting the Organization's Money

Churches are often accused of not conducting their business affairs in an efficient manner. It is charged that they do not pay their bills promptly, and that their members do not consider pledges made to the church in the light of a serious business obligation. A young people's group should be careful to see that all bills are paid promptly; in fact, it should run on a cash basis and not let bills pile up. Pledges made to Christian Endeavor Unions, to the church treasury, and to mission boards should be paid at the time that they are due, even if special methods need to be employed in order to get the money together.

There should be a similar earnestness in collecting the pledges or dues of members. Young people will be encouraged in the habit of shiftlessness and of petty dishonesty if the church bodies let them regard their pledges lightly. A promise made to the church or to a society is as serious a business matter as a bargain made with a shoe dealer. The society and the church are not fulfilling their moral obligations to young people if they do not make an earnest effort to have these financial promises met promptly and in full. This means that regular opportunity should be provided for the payment of these dues, either through collections or by the use of special envelopes.

When members are in arrears, some one specifically charged with that duty should make a personal appeal to each delinquent. This may be the task of the treasurer or of a collector. First, a general announcement may be made that some members have not paid up. If this announcement is made seriously and tactfully by the right person, it may produce results. If it does not, written or printed notices may be sent out, but it is better to approach the debtors in person. Scolding and impatience should be avoided; the matter should be discussed in a businesslike and friendly fashion. If the matter becomes a serious one in the sense that a large number are failing to meet their obligations, a discussion may be planned on such subjects as the following: "Some Petty Forms of Dishonesty," "A Young Person's Obligations to the Church," "The Importance of Keeping One's Word"; or the discussion may center wholly around the specific problem, "The Business Policy of Our Organization." It may be well to have a banker come in and talk to the group regarding the use of money. In such a case, the executive committee should inform him of the loose way in which some members regard their obligations to the church, asking him to emphasize the seriousness of a pledge or promise to pay, without, of course, making any direct reference to those who are in arrears.

This all requires skillful handling by persons who are able and tactful and well liked by the membership. The treasurer or collector should be a person who knows how to keep books or is willing to learn under expert supervision. He must be a person who is popular, otherwise he will have little success in appealing to delinquents. He must possess a combination of aggressiveness and tact. It has been said, half facetiously, that the collector should either be a young man, muscular and authoritative, or a charming girl who "has a way with her."

The books of the treasurer should be gone over every three or six months by the executive committee or some one appointed by them. For the protection of the treasurer himself and for the reputation of the society or department such an audit is necessary. If the group can secure the help of some trusted business man or woman in making the audit of the accounts, it may help them to a firmer financial basis and will usually enable them to proceed more wisely.

Materials Recommended for Further Study

Brown, Ina C. *Jesus' Teaching on the Use of Money.* Cokesbury Press.

Martin, Hugh. *Christ and Money.* Doubleday, Doran.

Morrill, Guy L. *Stewardship Stories.* Doubleday, Doran.

Stock, Harry T. *Young People and Money.* Congregational Education Society.

Wilson, Bert. *The Christian and His Money Problems.* Doran.

Trimble, Henry B. *The Christian Motive and Method in Stewardship.* Cokesbury Press.

CHAPTER IX

THE CHURCH AND RECREATION

ITS past mistakes remain to plague the church. Young people are still being led, through unenlightened adult criticisms, to the belief that the church is a " killjoy." The negative attitude of Puritanism and the thundering threats of nineteenth century revivalism have fastened upon modern Christianity a reputation which does not reflect the present temper of the church. For Protestantism was long ago liberated from that somberness of which it is accused. The social life which centers around the parish church has for a long time been a conspicuous phase of the community program. Adults now in middle life testify that the little church at the edge of the big city made one of the most wholesome contributions to their lives because it was for them, during adolescent years, the center of their social activities. During the present century, the recreational emphasis has been one of the four major notes in the religious education programs initiated by the churches, although the quality of the play programs has not always been high. It is now realized that it was not enough to inveigh against the degradations of commercialized amusements, that it does not suffice to invite young people to " the regular monthly social " and feel that we have thereby done our duty. The emphasis today is that entertainments under the auspices of the church shall be interesting, but that they must also produce fruits in Christian character.

Now that the church has made an honest endeavor to include fun in its program, it finds itself faced with a doubt as to whether in the coming day this field ought not to be vacated for agencies which can do the work more effectively. "To just what extent is it necessary for the church to conduct a recreational program?" is a query which many a local group may well discuss. There are so many community agencies, active and proficient in the leadership of recreation, that it would seem less necessary than formerly for the church to specialize in this field. If the church is to be given one night a week for its work with adolescents, should not that time be spent in some activity more significant than play? May we not be sure that the young people will engage in enough good times even though the church does not include them in its schedule? Or, if the church is to compete with the opportunities for pleasure now existing, must it not greatly enlarge its program and develop a leadership which is competent to conduct a range of activities comparable in quality and appeal with those under commercial or expert direction?

The answer to such questions cannot, of course, be given by a direct affirmative or negative to cover all cases. The local committee, in facing its duty, will discuss such matters as the following: Are the other agencies in the community equipped to carry on the type of educational recreation in which the church is interested? Are they willing to do it in such a way that the positive values about which the church is concerned shall be guaranteed? Will they agree that their program shall be free from those objectionable phases which vitiate the process of religious education? Will the classes and other units of church young people be permitted to carry on such social affairs as seem needful through the use of the community equipment?

The church does not want to multiply social affairs. It is more concerned with quality than anything else. It is also interested that the allegiance of young people to Christianity and the church shall not be weakened because the recreation of the community is in nonreligious or nonchurch control. Such control may be through a voluntary civic committee, or through a Christian Association. The church should insist that the philosophy underlying the community type of recreation shall be consonant with that in which religious educators believe; namely, that the play program shall re-create and strengthen and not dissipate the young people. It wants to make sure, too, that any real community equipment shall be available (in the event of complete coöperation by the churches) to the classes and departments of the church.

Why Recreation Should Be Included

There are several conceptions of the place of recreation in a program of religious education.

1. **Socials as bait.** Aside from the justification of the monthly social on the basis that "we have always had them," the idea of using them as bait to catch newcomers and to hold the feebly attached is, perhaps, the most common conception of the function of play. It is true that parties constitute one of the means by which a stranger may be introduced to the organization. He should there catch something of the real spirit of the fellowship, and it should be easy for him to establish that acquaintance which is necessary if he is to feel at home in the rest of the activities of the group. But there must be better reasons for socials than this.

2. **Play as a part of a project.** There are times when a social affair is the natural outgrowth of an enterprise in which the group is engaged. A society which has worked on a missionary project for Japanese children, collecting and making materials for a hospital, studying about the customs and ideas and needs of the Japanese, finds it quite the natural thing to have a party in which Japanese games and costumes are featured. The party serves a double purpose: it gives a vivid idea of the social life of the Japanese and it provides a wholesome period of fun for the young people.

3. Play as a means of achieving certain educational results in human character. Entirely aside from any specific study or service undertaking, play has its own contribution to make to the character development of the members of the group; it also influences the life of the social organism. Character results are best achieved through the natural means of social fellowship: common study and discussion, corporate worship, union in service, and social play. It is probable that the desirable traits of character cannot be attained except as young people have an opportunity to live their lives together in these four areas.

Behind all play there must be purpose: the purpose to develop Christian character, individually and in the group. The aims which underlie all of the educational process must apply in the development of the recreational plans. Not that every social must be planned with the intention of suddenly achieving some specific objective. To make of a given entertainment so definitely a didactic enterprise would probably kill the spontaneity and the joy which are the heart of play; it would defeat the specific objective and be the ruination of the recreational period itself. What is needed is so high a conception of the educational task of the church that nothing will be admitted to the social period which will be inane or questionable, and enough time will be spent in its preparation so that the social period will not be misspent but will produce genuine recreation. There are times when apparent lacks and needs are conspicuous. They constitute a " hot spot " for the educational leadership. Recreation, as well as worship or service or study, may be the means by which the emergency is met. Where, for example, cliquishness is apparent, the leader may arrange a type of social in which there is so complete a mixing of the young people that those who constitute the clique will of necessity have close and pleasing contacts with those who have been excluded — excluded, it may be, with no conscious intent.

Mr. Powell, in the Christian Quest pamphlet on recreation, calls attention to the following desirable outcomes of the social life within the church: (a) an unselfish type of coöperation; (b) courage and fearlessness and self-confidence; (c) expression of the creative spirit; (d) goodwill and the expression of friendliness; (e) honesty and fair play; (f) obedience or subjection of personal desires to that which is necessary for the good of the whole. Other character qualities suggested are: humility, joyousness, loyalty, purity, purposefulness, self-control.[1]

4. Play as an end in itself. While play, if it is wholesome, always contributes directly or indirectly to certain higher ends, it is its own justification. In this respect play is like worship and love and the reading of literature. Love makes for great good in the future; but love is a glorious experience in itself. Worship should develop habits and controls; but the experience of worship has value in itself if it is truly communion between man and God. The reading of great literature leaves its mark upon character, but the present enjoyment of noble prose or poetry is sufficient reason why we should spend time upon it. " A man should not eat his dinner simply for the sake of the added strength which he will thereby gain for the carrying on of his profession. A man should not go to a concert simply for the sake of fresh inspiration to carry on his appointed tasks. The dinner and the concert are goods in themselves and should be appreciated as such."[2] Naturally a controlling idea in the choice of a concert is that certain music is worth while, and in the eating of food that certain kinds of victuals build up and others tear down. But the enjoyment of a concert should not be ruined by the intrusion of the idea that this is going to " be good for me," or the enjoyment of a meal spoiled by a discourse upon vitamines and calories. So, too, with play. Fun is a legitimate experience in life.

[1] *Youth and Recreation,* by Warren T. Powell, pp. 10 ff. (Christian Quest pamphlet.)

[2] S. P. Lamprecht, in " The Journal of Philosophy," vol. 17, p. 562.

Planning the Program

1. **A year's schedule.** In the matter of recreation, it is well to think in terms of an entire year. It will be an excellent plan, if along with the study and service program for the young people's division (and of the various subsidiary organizations) there is printed the general plan for the social life. Where the group goes on a month-by-month basis, without a connected scheme and without either the variety or the unity of the whole being apparent, the young people are likely to underestimate the real contribution which the church plans to make to the social life.

2. **An intelligent and energetic committee.** In preparing the list of committees, the executive body sometimes thinks in terms of "important committees" and "less important" ones. Whether specifically so designated or not, the social committee is sometimes placed in the latter category. This is an error. Nothing is accomplished without hard work, and socials in particular require originality and laborious effort if they are to succeed. Just as young people find it easy to remain away from a discussion group if a single meeting has been inane, so they find it easy to stay away from the social affairs if they have had one experience of an unsatisfactory nature.

There should be a library of materials. Three or four books of the best suggestions, together with magazines which provide help, will constitute the minimum collection. Moreover, a record should be kept, either in card cases or in envelope files, of all successful programs. There should be a scrapbook or a file of games and stunts and similar types of recreational features; and this should constantly be enlarged by clippings from all sorts of current literature. Unless the committee works earnestly to build up such a collection of resource materials, it is pursuing a lazy course which will certainly eventuate in a series of mediocre programs. There will be no difficulty in finding recreational suggestions. The magazines are full of them. The publishers issue a constant stream of new books on the subject. The real task is to sift the worthwhile from the ordinary.

General publicity should be given to the whole year's program. The special committees should have the details of a particular social all worked out at least two weeks before the event, and at that time unique advertising of the entertainment should begin.

3. The importance of variety. The results of an informal questionnaire circulated among the young people in summer conferences in Nebraska, Florida, Connecticut, and Massachusetts, show that young people are interested in a great variety of amusements; that not all of our youth are as devoted to dancing and the movies as some of their elders suppose; and that one of their insistent demands is that social affairs shall contain varied types of entertainment. In listing the various possibilities, these conscientious and loyal leaders of Christian young people's groups said that they considered church socials the least interesting of all. If this is true of those who continue to attend them, how much chance has the average church social of tempting that great group on the outside who need a wholesome type of recreation, such as the religious organization should provide? If there is any secret by which the play programs of Christian groups can be made thrilling and attractive, at the same time being consistent with the highest Christian purposes, it is to be found in these words: *variety and hard work.* There have been enough demonstrations of church groups which have succeeded through a loyalty to these ideas to assure any local group that it is possible to make its program very popular with the liveliest and most worthwhile young people in the community.

The social committee will need to include such types of features as the following:

Sports	Stunts
Humor	Brain puzzlers
Drama	Seasonable events

4. Where shall social affairs be held? In this matter, as in the content of the program, variety is an important element.

In the church. If there are social quarters in the church edifice, it is likely that most of the indoor parties will be held there. Where the equipment is very limited, there may be a division of opinion as to what should be done in the room dedicated to worship. In general, there is wisdom in reserving the auditorium of the church for services of a distinctly worship type. Whether this idea should be tenaciously adhered to in the one-room church is an open question which every church should decide for itself. Indeed, one of the most valuable subjects for thoughtful investigation concerns the church, the church building, reverence, the relation between play and worship and "living the Christian life." Out of such a study, it may be agreed that the auditorium of the church should not be used for play purposes, although a contrary decision may be reached. Wherever the church equipment makes it possible, much of the social life should center in this building. There is an important psychological asset in developing the thought of the church building as the center for play and friendship as well as for worship.

Out-of-doors. In most groups, it is well to hold from a third to a half of the social events outdoors. Some of the parties will include outdoor features and will at the same time feature indoor amusement.

In a community hall. Where the Y.M.C.A. or Y.W.C.A. or the community itself has recreational equipment which the church lacks, use should be made of these facilities. This is quite commonly done in cities where the classes of various churches engage in competitive athletic events. But in addition to these class affairs, there is need of great social events which will include all the young people of a given church, of the several churches of a denomination, and even of all the Christian churches. On some of these occasions, the Christian Associations and churches should combine whole-heartedly in planning programs which will be second to none in the community experience of the entire year.

In homes. One of the great joys of a generation ago was the occasional evening spent in a home, where hilarious and joyful parties were held. It is important that the church should lead in this "back to the home movement." The home needs again to become a social center for young life. Many of the dangerous tendencies of the day could be changed if the homes were again made attractive to the young people.

5. Social affairs should re-create. Our rapidly moving modern life, with its search for new thrills, dissipates the mental power, the moral reserve, and the nervous energy of old and young; that is to say, it is un-Christian. It is likewise immoral. A test of the Christian type of recreation is that it renews or re-creates. All amusement produces one of these two results: it leaves the participant stronger or weaker, better or worse, renewed or dissipated.

The church is in competition with a host of commercialized entertainments which leave the emotions frayed and fill the mind with imaginations which can only bring harm. They hold a charm for youth, at least for a while. They provide thrills. Thrills must also be a part of the church program, but they must be of the type that last, of the sort which appeal to the best that there is in one rather than to the wildest side of human nature. Hundreds of adults will testify to the cumulative joy which has come from friendships made at church parties. Hundreds of conscientious young people are troubled over the base tendencies of much of the community social life. Yet they are eager to experience that fullness of life which is the proper possession of old and young. They would grasp eagerly at a varied and lively program of recreation engineered by the church if it provided those thrills which come from wholesome mingling in play. Excessive release of the animal spirit can but injure youth; the repression of it does no good. Young people need self-expression in play — as they need it in discussion and worship and service. The question is: What kind of self-expression, how much? Does it build up the inner life, or does it soil it? Does it re-create or does it dissipate?

6. The class or society by itself. Some social events should be confined to the particular unit of young people's life, such as the class or society. The Scout activities constitute the major element in the program of a class organized as a troop. Probably most societies will want a social each month. This is legitimate and proper, but it must not be the only social fellowship among young people. No single agency must be given complete right of way, for the needs of the whole are more important than the desires of any part. It is not enough for a class to have its fellowship wholly by itself; it needs to realize that it is a part of the whole, and the play life is a natural means of bringing about this realization. The program of recreation for any given year should provide certain events and dates for fun for each agency by itself; it should likewise schedule other programs for the whole group of young people in the church.

7. The entire age division. Just how many socials the classes should hold by themselves and how many should include the entire department is a matter which depends upon local needs. In this connection there arises the question as to whether the departments can well mingle for any type of social affair. Usually it is better for the intermediates to have their parties by themselves, but there should be at least one occasion during the year when they join with seniors in play. If we think of the church as a family institution, it is essential that in every phase of its life there be some opportunity for the old and the young to cooperate and share common experiences.

8. Play as a project of service. In most communities there are groups who are shut off from the opportunity to play. Some young people's departments could render a fine piece of service by providing a social time for some of these groups, and it would result in an experience of genuine joy for those undertaking it. The following are illustrations of what is meant:

A party or picnic for juniors.

A picnic for the very old, at which refreshments, transportation and program are furnished by the young people. Care should be taken not to make it too strenuous for the guests.

A party for children from poorer neighborhoods, either in connection with some holiday or at some other season of the year.

A picnic for mothers who have small children, the young people dividing their activities: some of them caring for the children, the others "running" the picnic.

A dinner and party for parents, either in connection with Mother and Daughter or Father and Son Week, or wholly separate from these occasions. If this is arranged, the young people should do all of the work: arranging the tables, preparing the food, serving the meal, furnishing the program, and cleaning up after the dinner is over.

9. Recreation as a study project. Some of the most perplexing problems of adolescent life center around social contacts. Many of the most baffling "personal problems" have their origin in parties and leisure-time activities. No more useful study could be carried out than that which evaluates the various types of recreation, which considers the character results which come from them, and which then eventuates in a code of conduct which Christian young people should follow in their social contacts. The project, of course, will not be complete unless the Christian young people who have pursued the investigation organize their resources to establish that type of recreational and leisure-time activity which accords with the principles which have been approved.

10. Study of play as a missionary enterprise. In missionary programs almost everything has been studied; such as religious beliefs, social conditions, educational needs, health, etc. One of the most significant features of any nation's life is the amount and character of its play. To study the needs of foreign youth (or of certain of our American children) in terms of their play, would reveal their life as few other approaches would. Out of such an investigation would grow a series of programs which might involve the dramatization of the life of these people, a series of social events in which their games were played, and an enterprise of friendliness which would include an exchange of correspondence and some act of Christian service.

11. Interdenominational recreational activities. In many communities there are competitive recreational activities between boys' and girls' classes of the various churches, in basket ball, aquatic events, and other athletic features. This is the beginning of a community-wide consciousness on the part of the Christian young people. But it is not enough. In addition to these competitive events there must be coöperative or union fellowships in play. If the Christian young people of a small town, or of a neighborhood in a large city, were to combine in two or three great social affairs every year, they would contribute toward the coming of the unity of Christendom more than they could predict. Not only that; they would receive such publicity as few of our church socials can receive at present, a publicity which would give status to Christian recreation which it very much needs.

Troublesome Questions

Questions asked by young people at conferences and institutes reveal a widespread perplexity regarding three main types of controversial subjects. The author does not desire to fix the minds of local leaders in any particular mold; indeed, he would feel rewarded if he helped to unfix the prejudices of old and young. It is his hope that adults and young people may be encouraged to a frank facing of concrete issues. It is expensive folly for local and national leaders to ignore issues, trivial though they may be thought to be, which are exaggerated to genuine importance in the minds of youth. Trivialities are the cause of many of our most serious misunderstandings.

1. Shall we dance at church parties? This question is asked at practically every conference. Usually it comes in the form of a protest against adults who have refused the permission which the young people think they should be given. Why is this so insistent a query? There appear to be three reasons. The first is that young people almost universally dance at school and other parties; it is a recognized, if not *the* recognized, form of community pleasure. In the second place, the expressed or supposed prohibition of dancing at church parties seems to many young people an unreasonable interference with their rights; the unwillingness of youth to be suppressed by any form of prohibition which it does not understand and with which it does not agree finds sharp expression at this point. The third fact is that increasingly churches in almost every city and of almost every communion are including some dancing in their recreational schedules.

In attempting to reach a common understanding of duty in this matter, the first point to be studied is this: Do the adult members of the church still regard dancing as a sin or a near-sin, and if so, is their opinion well founded? Do these same adults forbid dancing at school parties and community entertainments, for the children of their homes? That is to say, the first question deals only with the rightness or wrongness of dancing itself. The chief contention of those who oppose dancing is that it places boys and girls during a long period of time and to the accompaniment of music which affects both the body and the emotions, in physical attitudes such that the animal spirits are almost certainly aroused to a dangerous degree. If actual sexual excesses do not follow, imaginations and desires have inevitably been aroused or stimulated so as to work injury to mind or body. No one can deny this possibility; that the dance has often furnished the setting or the occasion for a wild release of passion is an incontrovertible fact.

It must, however, be remembered that these young people are human, that they possess certain desires and impulses, that these are not wholly bad, and that continued attempts at the repression of all emotions and passions may do more serious injury than a controlled direction of them. A form of physical expression, under wholesome auspices, in the bright light of a public hall, with genuine joy in the social fellowship, frequently saves a young man or woman from those excesses which occur so commonly in more protected places. Dancing as a form of social recreation may be a means of preventing private dissipation. The whole matter is a proper subject for study on the part of the adults, study in the light of scientific knowledge. After the adults have gained real information on the subject, it may be a matter for common discussion with the young people. In any event, it will require clear thinking and sane judgment. Decisions must not be made on the basis of blind prejudice or of unreasoned loyalty to tradition. Neither should genuine principles be compromised to meet the demands of a younger generation which itself knows little of what is involved. And in thinking of the dangers which lurk in the dance, it might be well for parents to ask themselves this question: If it is wrong for boys and girls to be placed in close propinquity at a public dance, should not every parent hesitate a long time before he permits an automobile to be used by boys and girls together?

The second question comes directly to the matter of dancing under church auspices. Suppose the parents permit dancing at school affairs. Shall they approve it as a part of the church program? Shall it be allowed within the church property? Any honest attempt at decision will include such questions as these: Has the church a parish house where such a pastime may be indulged in without doing violence to the conception of the church building as a place of worship? Are there so many people in the church who conscientiously disapprove that it would not be playing fair with the total church family to introduce dancing over their protest? To what extent should the young people be penalized in order to satisfy the whims of their elders? Will dancing in the church improve the moral tone of neighborhood life, or will the social life of the church be injured by its inclusion? Will the result be repeated which was experienced in a case where a church installed a pool table in order to keep boys from frequenting the pool halls? The boys learned to play in the church and then spent more time than ever at the public halls. Whatever the decision may be, it must be the fruit of intelligent discussion carried on with the single desire of doing that which is right. Such a discussion must be participated in by representatives of the various age-groups, and with full agreement that the church belongs to all — old and young — and that any decision must seek to meet the needs of the entire group.

If it is decided that dancing at church affairs should be allowed, it must be recognized that as many problems have been raised as have been solved. The solution of the first difficulty may be the means of overcoming the others, but not necessarily. Is the dancing at the church to be just like that at nonchurch parties; is it to be so tame that it will appeal to none of the spirited young people; is it to lower the level of the whole church life? The same cautions apply here as in all other forms of recreation: the church must not sink to the level of commercial forms of pleasure; it has the

duty of trying to raise all forms of community entertainment; any worthwhile recreational program will require as careful planning and as hard work as other forms of diversion. Then, care must be taken that dancing does not become the only or the major form of social pastime. Certainly, out of a dozen parties not more than one or two should be dances; or, if some dancing is desired at most of the parties, it should constitute only a minor phase of each evening's entertainment. While the dance is in progress other very attractive games should be provided for those who do not dance. The games which follow the dance should be of the most thrilling character and should be heartily participated in by all. Where dances are magnified, there is real danger that there will be a growing class consciousness between the dancers and the "wall-flowers." In order that the program shall provide genuine recreational and educational features, there must be elements which require mental alertness as well as physical participation. Dancing requires little intelligence. It is a diversion which does not necessarily add much to the mental content of the young people, and every program of recreation should contain some features which sharpen the wits and refresh the mind.

2. **Shall there be social features in connection with the Sunday night program?** The basis for this query is found in two directions: a large number of young people's groups have a luncheon and social period preceding their discussion, and many other groups feel that the success of their Sunday evening meetings might be guaranteed if refreshments and games were made a regular feature.

The most common plan is to have a simple lunch, prepared successively by different committees of young people, followed either by a short game period or a half hour of social fellowship. Sometimes this policy is carried out weekly, in other cases it is a bi-weekly or monthly event. Objection is sometimes made by adults on two grounds: it is not right to use the church for entertainment purposes on Sunday, and it is "too bad that you have to feed people in order to get them out." With the second idea, the writer is in sympathy; but, after all, these are young people. We adults may prefer to eat at home. It is possible that we attend church functions as eagerly when there are to be no refreshments as when there is to be something to eat. But young people like to eat.

They like to sit around and talk to each other. They enjoy games. Certainly we should not try to make them old before their time, and our own inclination should not be interposed to spoil what may be a two-hour period of genuine Christian fellowship.

As to the first objection, that it is not right to have pleasurable events on Sunday — again, the group should think this through together in the light of their understanding of the spirit of Jesus. It would be fatal to try to bring back the traditional Scotch Sabbath — a day on which smiles were frowned upon. Is it any more wrong to laugh and eat on Sunday than on Saturday, in a church than in a home? Do we prefer to have "couples" eat in restaurants rather than in the church building? Is it not a part of the task of religious education to make of the whole life a religious process, and will not the religious spirit seem a much more natural and vital thing if it pervades the period of play as well as the session of worship and discussion? Is it not true to life itself to combine play and study and devotion in a single unit? There is danger of overdoing the social feature on Sunday. In planning and carrying out the complete schedule, it should be made very clear that the whole Sunday program is carried out with a religious intent. The games to be played will necessarily be carefully selected, and of a somewhat different type from those which might form the content of a week-night program, but they must not be of the sort which remind spirited young people of tiddledewinks. It is all a matter of balance and a "sense of the fitness of things." It will be found that the young people will be as ready to make concessions and adjustments as their elders are.

A genuine opportunity comes to the Christian forces of a community in throwing open the doors of the homes, by regular arrangement, to the young people for a couple of hours following the evening service. This is the time when they are tempted to patronize commercial entertainments or to indulge in questionable private practices. Some of the discussion and worship meetings may also be held in homes, the play period following naturally afterward. To those adults who will criticize with a senseless squeamishness, the question should be put as to what the alternative of such a social fellowship is likely to be!

A third combination of the recreational with the more distinctly "spiritual" is that which centers around a Sunday afternoon hike. What can be more impressive by way of a consecration service than a vesper meeting at twilight? The hike itself is an excellent form of Christian fellowship. The natural forms of play which would follow for an hour or two before sunset would certainly be in keeping with Jesus' attitude toward the Sabbath. The picnic supper would be another means of cementing the family comradeship which should exist in all young people's groups.

Basic in this whole program is the question as to what is happening to the minds of the young people. Are they coming to think of the church as standing firmly for the best values in life, as an instrument by which the life-enriching spirit of religion is being mediated to all days and all phases of human experience? Or are they thinking of it in terms of a somber institution to which they may flee in times of distress or to which they may resort during their serious moods, and one from which they must "shy off" when they are in the midst of the "celebration of life"? Is there not, after all, an identity of essential spirit in play and worship? And must not the church help young people to see this connection, rather than intensify the opinion that the church stands for worship and is against the natural expression of the spirit of play?

3. Shall we have chaperones? "Of course," say the adults. "Why?" counter young rebels. What is the answer? Why do the adults believe in chaperones? Is it not largely that they may police the party so that "nothing will happen"? Then the young people ask, "Can't they trust us?" Many an elder will be moved to reply, "No: we aren't sure that we can." Nor is the adult all wrong. But the less confidence the older generation has in the younger, the greater the cause for fear. Adults must divest themselves of the idea that chaperones should in all cases be provided in order to keep wild youth in check.

Ask any young people's group, — "Suppose you have a choice of the adults who are to attend your parties, what objection will you have to their presence? Why should you resent having a few older folks present, if you are permitted to invite those whom you want?" Will they object? As often as not, the reply will be somewhat after the following manner: "Oh, we haven't had any trouble with chaperones. They have always been fair to us. And the church has let us choose the ones we want. It's just the idea that we're opposed to." What idea? Press them further, and it appears that it is the word "chaperone" that proves the stumbling-block. Instead of having chaperones let the young people invite several "patrons," "patronesses," or "guests," and the difficulty is solved. It is a psychological problem more than anything else. The young people do not want to be watched, but they do not insist upon being left entirely to themselves. They are glad to have adults present whom they trust and who

trust them, but they want them to be invited as guests rather than as necessary guards. It is a perfectly logical desire. It represents exactly the idea which should prevail in a church, as in a home: old and young are united in the enjoyment of the common family life.

If the church has considered well its own character, the problem of chaperones should not arise. If it is truly a family institution, the youthful members will not be eternally suspicious. If young people have served on important committees with adults and have worked with them in all manner of tasks, they will look upon the older people as comrades, because the adults themselves have maintained a warmth of friendliness and understanding. If the young people's department or society has had counselors, chosen jointly by the church itself and by the adolescent group, the division between old and young will not be magnified. Guests at parties will be as naturally and heartily welcomed as advisers are at the discussion sessions, and they will probably be the same persons. Questions regarding proper types of games will be solved as calmly and considerately as any other phase of the group program. But unless this essential attitude has been established — that of a church as a genuine family of kindred spirits of all ages — not much can be done to overcome the idea that adults are always lurking behind corners to criticize, command or condemn.

Material Recommended for Further Study

Bancroft, Jessie H. *Games for the Playground, Home, School and Gymnasium.* Macmillan.

Bowen, Wilbur P. *The Theory of Organized Play.* Barnes.

Davies, J. W. F. *Out of Doors with Youth.* University of Chicago Press.

Gates, Herbert W. *Recreation and the Church.* University of Chicago Press.

Geister, Edna. *Ice Breakers.* Doubleday, Doran.

Gulick, Luther H. *A Philosophy of Play.* Association Press.

Harbin, Elvin O. *Phunology.* Cokesbury Press.

Heaton, Kenneth L. *Character Building Through Recreation.* University of Chicago Press.

La Porte, William R. *Handbook of Games and Programs.* Abingdon Press.

——. *Recreational Leadership of Boys.* Methodist Book Concern.

Miller, Catherine A. *Stunt Night To-Night.* Doubleday, Doran.

Moxcey, Mary E. *Physical Health and Recreation for Girls.* Methodist Book Concern.

Powell, Warren T. *Recreational Leadership for Church and Community.* Methodist Book Concern.

——. *Youth and Recreation.* International Council of Religious Education. (Christian Quest booklet.)

Richardson, Norman E. *The Church at Play.* Abingdon Press.

Rohrbough, Lynn. *Handy.* Church Recreation Service.

Parties (magazine). Dennison Manufacturing Co., Framingham, Mass.

CHAPTER X

THE WIDER FELLOWSHIP

NO man lives to himself if he is truly a social being. No class or club of young people is sufficient to itself. Religious bodies, like all other groups of human beings, need that inspiration which comes through a community of interests and a sharing in common ventures. Some of the most active societies and clubs, having detached themselves from existing community and national fellowships, have awakened to a sense of loss. It is not that they are poor intellectually, or that they need the steering hand of an outsider to keep them steady, but they are outside of the main movement of the stream. They have longed to exchange experiences with their comrades in Christian living. They are aware that only as religious groups coöperate in significant tasks are they knit together in that unity of spirit which is essential if the Kingdom of God is to come upon the earth. In order to maintain a maximum of interest, to provide full educational opportunity, and to enable the youth of a community to make that expression in service which is commensurate with their abilities, it is important that the young people of a church shall be related to similar groups in other churches, both within the community and in the wider areas.

There are, in the first place, the natural means of fellowship provided by the denominations, some of which have organizations of their own young people, sometimes extending down into the local churches, and in other cases existing only as federations or associations which tie the local groups of all names together behind common aims. Almost every national church, whether it has organizations bearing distinctive names or not, is desirous of uniting its youth in common endeavor for certain specified ends. True, these denominational plans are sometimes lamentably inadequate — they are wooden, artificial, far removed from the life experiences of the sophisticated youth of some parishes. They too often proceed from the theories of adults, schooled in the verbiage of systematic theology or committed to the promotional schemes of statistically minded church boards, unlearned in the discoveries of modern psychology, and utterly unacquainted with the thinking of twentieth-century adolescence.

Competent leaders in the local field often find these materials ill-adapted to their needs; they are tempted to ignore all denominational programs and meetings. This is as bad a policy as that of taking blindly everything that is "handed down from above." Excessive individualism is as harmful as the undiscriminating "yessing" of everything which issues from a denominational scriptorium. The only educational process is that which considers well what is offered by able educational leadership — denominational, interdenominational, undenominational, local, and national — separating the valuable from the unworthy. This will supplement the plans and methods locally created. Such a program will represent the sound thinking of many men of many views. By such a procedure the denominational offering will be modified, essentially accepted, or largely rejected in favor of something better suited to the parish needs.

Most of us are impatient with our denominational divisions. We are committed to Christian union; but we cannot be foolish enough to ignore the fact that divisions do exist, that almost all of our local churches are related to a wider and yet restricted fellowship. If young people are to be trained as workers, it will be as workers within churches that bear recognized labels. This should not disqualify them from being equally good workers within churches of other names. We need to grow our leaders for service in the churches which exist as well as for those that are to be — and the churches which exist are denominational. Conferences and organizations bearing the names of the national churches have their weaknesses: they tend to promote an institutionalized mind and an unreasoned loyalty to a part of the church, and they often rest content with gross ignorance regarding the church as a whole. An overemphasis upon institutes and upon certain artificial fellowships within the denomination must cramp the creative spirit of youth and delay the coming of Christian unity. But there is a danger in the other direction, which has been intensified by well-meaning speakers at undenominational student conferences: it is that of cutting the loyalty to the church universal by exaggerating the sins of the churches in particular. While we work for the unified church, a church which will provide freedom of thought and action for all of its units as well as for each individual, we must be careful not to alienate young people from those existent church fellowships of which they are a part — the only church fellowships which are now possible. Blame the leadership of national bodies as we may for their obscurantism, it must be said that (with a few notable exceptions) almost all of the forward-looking program elements and materials which are today being offered to our churches are coming from the leaders within the denominations — materials which are issued either by a single national church or by several in coöperation.

It is seldom, if ever, enough for groups of young people to be bound together within the fellowship of a single communion. Boys and girls are together in school and at play. They are surrounded by the same temptations and opportunities. They need the same chance for personal development. They ought to engage in constructive enterprises which call for the combined thought and energy of all. The churches are arch sinners if they keep them separated in religious quests and ventures. Can it be that the churches are less interested in presenting a united force of youth in combat against community evils than the community itself is in organizing adolescence against illiteracy and ignorance? For the sake of the common citizenry youth must be united. No real impression can be made upon the social situation and upon human relationships unless there are a united intention and a concentrated effort to establish desirable habits of living. If the level of neighborhood life is to be raised to that point which Christians desire when they pray the Lord's prayer, it will be through the leadership of Christians — and this requires the mobilization of all Christian life. One of the scandals of present-day religion is the fact that people who are very much alike, who profess to serve the same Christ, who are committed to the establishment of the Kingdom of God, are held to a narrow sectarianism by prejudice and tradition — a sectarianism which almost always gives the appearance of being more interested in the success of a part than it is in the accomplishments of the whole. Adult leaders must not be content to *allow* youth to coöperate; it is the part of Christian duty to see that every available opportunity for such coöperation is made possible.

Agencies of Coöperation

Two opposite tendencies are apparent today: one toward an intensified denominationalism and the other toward a wider interdenominationalism. This shows itself particularly in the national field, where churches are increasing their facilities for the creation and promotion of denominational programs, and the interchurch bodies are extending the range of their service, adding to their endowments, and enlarging their personnel. It is possible that these two tendencies are not contradictory. It may be that we are just realizing the size of our task and are using every possible means to develop program elements and to make them available in the field so that together we shall not fail too completely. But there is grave danger in this double development. National leaders, denominational and nondenominational, have not yet squarely faced the issues involved in our present organizational complexity. There has as yet been no thorough and unprejudiced and determined consideration of the question as to where denominational activity should end and where interdenominational efforts should have the right of way.

If denominations continue to promote programs, each built by its own leadership without regard to the common needs of the young people of all of the churches or the offerings of sister communions, each more nicely particularized than heretofore, we shall be headed toward a more complete failure in Christian education than has yet been recorded. Not that diversity of program elements, of curriculum materials, is undesirable. But the single-viewed promotion of sectarian programs by a dozen leading churches will bring added confusion and increased division into community and church life. If all of these churches could agree to center their emphasis upon common needs, then undertake to build together during a period of five years as much of this common program as possible, leaving to the individual churches only those matters which represent fundamental theological or organizational differences, we should discover such a renaissance in young people's work as has come but once or twice in American religious history. Then the critical world would have some evidence that we mean what we say when we utter smooth words regarding coöperation. The first real need is a more determined resolution to face together the fields of coöperative effort. Do the denominations really believe in coöperation?

1. Denominational programs. The attitude of the national churches is that the young people are " our young people " — the members of the classes and societies of this particular denomination. Because this is true, the national body is under the necessity of providing such help for these adolescents as coincides with the church theories as to what is good and necessary. The home and the church are the primary agencies of religious education. Civic or community agencies cannot serve in lieu of these two; they may supplement the program, but they cannot be the responsible organizations. This requires, in the first place, that the denomination shall have a specialized staff for the various age-groups. This staff will develop a program, based upon the distinctive aims believed in by the church. There will be promotional literature, curriculum elements, organizations through which the work may become effective. Thus, as denominations have been able to find financial resources, they have begun to do for their young people those things which seemed necessary — and this has usually included the building of a complete program, from a to z, without any real consideration of what other denominations have done or are planning — except in the graded lessons.

No national church is over-staffed in the field of young people's work. None of these bodies can keep up with the demands which are being made upon them. Not less but more needs to be done to help local leaders. But most denominations are using their staff uneconomically. Has the time not come when each national secretary can do for all of the others many things which will not need to be done separately by each? Is it not time that through the International Council of Religious Education (which is " the denominations at work in the field of religious education "), young people's leaders should create together many common elements of program, thus relieving each denomination of doing everything for itself? Should not the state councils of religious education be means of promoting these common program elements and of serving also each denominational church in the spirit that its leadership desires? Ought not the denominational representatives within a state first bear responsibility for their own churches in the total program of religious education, and should they not then be recognized as a part of the state council staff, together promoting the entire program of all of the churches — the state council program being the program of the denominations within that field? A beginning has been made in the Christian Quest pamphlets (valuable suggestions for leaders in young people's work), but we must go far beyond that: we must build together the actual program elements for young people's work, and these, being the creation of the denominations jointly, will be the chief promotional interest of the leaders of the national churches and of the interdenominational bodies. Otherwise, we shall have not only a multiplicity of denominational emphases but to these will be added a distinct interdenominational program, which coincides with none of the denominational plans and which confuses the local churches of every communion.

2. **Interdenominational developments.** Despite the grave possibilities inherent in the new emphasis upon denominational programs, there are two hopeful signs: one is that national secretaries meet together so frequently in workshop fashion that they are subjected to that education which comes from the sharing of ideas and ideals. They are consequently being drawn together more closely in purpose and program. Then, too, local workers, regardless of denomination, are feeling a new freedom and responsibility for building their own plans, selecting and using whatever materials seem best, regardless of their source. Congregational churches are using much Methodist material, and *vice versa*. Church unity must be achieved through a movement which comes from both ends: from the secretarial "top," and from the community up. And this unity is coming more quickly than most of us realize.

First, there are character-growth agencies which are not strictly religious. At the intermediate age, particularly, our boys and girls are organized into a variety of popular clubs and troops. These, frequently, have a community character and are not distinctly related to the churches. They are founded upon noble purposes, but they are not regarded as religious education agencies; indeed, some of them would object to being thought of as Christian organizations. They are rendering fine service to hundreds of thousands of youth. They win the deep loyalty of these young people, a loyalty which often overshadows their interest in the church. Against this the church must not protest, unless it has offered a scheme of religious education which is better and as interesting as this extra-church program.

The problem of integrating such programs is widespread and insistent. The only possible means by which a Christian solution can be found is through conference on the part of all the responsible leaders. People who "put their feet under a table," determined to talk together frankly and long enough, will eventually find a solution for all their difficulties. The will to coöperate is the prerequisite.

a. The community interest resident in these inclusive organizations must be developed; the church interest must also be conserved. A church which interferes with the genuine expression of the unity of youth within a community is an agent of disruption and not of construction. A character-growth agency which does not try at all points to foster the religious training of youth, through the churches of their choice, lacks those qualifications which are essential if it is to have the confidence of religious people.

b. It is unwise to think too much in terms of prerogatives and of precedence. Until representatives of all groups come to think in terms of young life, and of the possibility of building together a plan which will serve all best, they cannot make much progress toward a community enterprise which will have saving power.

c. The leaders of the community organizations should be deeply religious persons, actively related to the churches, if these agencies expect the coöperation or even the approval of the churches. "Good character" is not enough, religious character and interest are demanded; for the church cannot look with equanimity upon any program which asks the weekday loyalty of intermediates unless the leadership is such as will commend the religious life and encourage a devotion to the kingdom of God. If such religious leadership is not available or is not desired by the community organization (a religious leadership which does not teach sectarianism or instruct in doctrine, but which is clearly devoted to the things of God and is loyally attached to a church) — it may be the duty of the churches to develop together some other means of weekday character education which will be integrated with the local programs of religious training.

d. In no case should the community organization set up schedules which conflict with the essential plans and the fixed arrangements of the churches. Specifically, Scout leaders should not take boys on hikes nor should they announce any other meeting on Sunday at times which are recognized as church hours. The churches should be equally conscientious in keeping free those nights which are the regular troop hours.

e. The responsible religious education leaders of the churches should be regular members of the committee which oversees the work of the community agency. The church should show the same recognition to the leaders of the community activities, by giving them membership upon young people's councils and similar program-planning bodies.

f. When a common agreement is reached, the several forces should join hands in promoting the major elements of the total program. Such unanimity is desirable as will lead all concerned to think in terms of *one great program* rather than to maintain the idea that there are many programs which come together at several points.

Second, there are the undenominational and interdenominational agencies of religious education. The distinction which is usually made between these two types is that the undenominational is a separate corporation controlled by a board of directors not responsible to the denominations, free to conduct the entire program without regard to the desires of church bodies. In some cases, no denominational representation of any sort is sought. There is manifestly a serious danger in this kind of proceeding: the young people of every church are lured by the undenominational leadership, key pastors are urged to send their best adolescents to share the training offered by the agency. The training provided may, of course, be of the very highest type. The local constituency needs to be informed of every good method and material made available by any leader or agency — official or free-lance. But unless there is a corresponding contact by the adult leadership of the local parish, and a serious effort by both the conference leaders and the local workers to relate what goes on in these undenominational conferences and camps to the actual local situation within a given church, much of this training misses the mark, and we have confusion more confused.

Some of these undenominational agencies seek the representation of the various denominations on their boards, but they do the selecting themselves. Such appointees do not, of course, represent the denomination. They may not even represent the denominational viewpoint. They are frequently chosen because they are pastors of influential churches. Seldom are they acquainted with educational ideals, either those approved by their own denomination or those accepted by such an agency as the International Council of Religious Education. They, therefore, not infrequently give approval to plans issued in behalf of the undenominational body which run absolutely counter to the beliefs of the recognized educational staffs of the churches, plans which will be promoted among the young people of these same churches. Far from insisting that there should be a single system of religious education recommended for all churches of one or all denominations, we believe in the absolute freedom of the local church to make its program. But at the same time a protest must be entered against the multiplication of program-making bodies which issue for church young people plans and proposals that have the sanction of no national church board. Pastors and local leaders are already caught in a maze of conflicting schemes. If the undenominational religious agencies expect to have free access to the young people of the churches, they should become interdenominational in character.

An interdenominational agency is not " another " organization. It is the denominations at work together. Its board and committees are made up of the official educational leaders of the churches with the collaboration of other experts. Its object should be to present plans and program elements which represent the united thinking of the church leaders — both in the local and the national fields. This interdenominational body should help each communion to acquaint its own constituency with the ideas which are distinctive to it. It should serve also as a clearing house of information regarding materials and methods, without regard to their source. Each national church, on the other hand, should serve as a means by which the total program developed by the co-operating churches is promoted. The interchurch agency should be the total church at work; thus it will not overshadow the parts; the parts cannot do their best work apart from the whole.

For the sake of unity, for that unity which believes in diversity, it must be urged that undenominational religious agencies which seek to work with church people should become interdenominational in their set-up. Otherwise the undenominational body is in the process of becoming another denomination, and those who pose as the friends of non-sectarianism establish a new sectarianism. This is not a false fear. It is the expression of a well-considered judgment which corresponds to the facts in many communities, all the way from the intermediate age-group up through the university student population.

a. The Christian Associations. These two organizations are doing some of the finest work which is being accomplished for the boys and girls of the intermediate age. The program includes the attractive "activity phases" and also emphasizes the centrality of religion. Many churches would do well to relate their church-school classes to the programs provided by the associations. Whether this can be accomplished depends upon the breadth of mind and the genuine coöperative spirit of the local workers — ministers, church-school leaders, association secretaries. Occasionally there is serious complaint because the association woos the young people away from the church edifice and provides such excellent facilities in the community building. Rather than resent such a procedure, the church leader will do well to try to make an arrangement whereby the activities in the association property may be integrated with the religious education enterprises of the churches. It is a common experience that association leaders are delighted to offer to the church school the use of the gymnasium and other rooms on designated nights for the class activities. This is exactly the kind of coöperation which should be desired. Moreover, the Girl Reserve program and the Pioneer program are excellent plans which may be used coöperatively by the churches and the associations.

The church which stands off in sullen and jealous criticism of the success of the associations needs to resort to a period of humility and prayer. The Christian Association which expects to be truly a Christian Association must see to it that its secretaries are men and women who are deeply interested in religion, closely affiliated with the churches, and concerned with strengthening rather than competing with the religious education activities within the church school. Greater progress is perhaps being made in integrating the activities of the churches and associations at the intermediate age than at any other. Certainly much more of this same spirit needs to prevail in the university field. The apparent unwillingness of church workers and association secretaries actually to make a united approach — united in spirit and not merely tolerant of a paper scheme — to the total campus religious situation is one of the most notorious evidences of sectarianism in America — sectarianism within church denominations and within the associations.

b. Christian Endeavor Unions. Throughout America, for many years, Christian Endeavor unions have carried on aggressive programs which enlisted the time and money of the young people of many churches. They have accomplished great good, but there have been many criticisms of their activities. The charge is made that there is too much organizational propaganda and too little educational content. At the same time, it must be recognized that the leaders of this movement have been constantly and meticulously careful to stress the local church as the organization which deserves the first loyalty of its membership. "For Christ and the church" is the motto which the society has kept to the forefront.

Pastors and adult counselors frequently ask, "Is it worth while for our young people to go to union meetings and state conventions?" The answer, of course, can be given by no one except the local leadership. If it is found to be true, as charged, that the sessions contribute little help to the local society, that the meetings are directed to the adult mind and not to the adolescent, if educational methods are wholly ignored, if it seems necessary to unlearn much of what was emphasized at these sessions, if both platform and group meetings are inconsistent with the thought of a scientific world, then the local group should face honestly the question as to whether it pays to maintain the fellowship.

In reaching a decision, account should be taken of such arguments as the following: If the educational standards are not high, it is better to spend time and money for those fellowships which produce more in the way of gain. If the organization develops an inferiority complex, because platform leaders tell the young people that they must believe and do what they really cannot believe and do not feel moved to do, the permanent effect is likely to be bad. If the union activities seem to be trivial, it is better to devote time to those things which are truly significant. If the ideals of the denomination are vitiated by the union program, there can be little advantage in attending. On the other hand, what is the reason for fellowship? Is it for ourselves alone, or is it to provide help for others? In order to have helpful relationships, must we agree upon details? Is the superior feeling toward the union merely an aristocratic offishness or an intellectual snobbishness? Is it possible that by joining the union and entering heartily into its program the activities of the organization may be raised to that level which the local society approves? By holding aloof, is a given organization shutting itself off from participation in community enterprises which deserve the support of all loyal Christians? Does the fact that the local society bears the name of the national movement obligate it to share in its wider program?

c. Young people's councils. The International Council of Religious Education is the outstanding agency of interdenominational effort in the whole range of Christian education. The state councils are — at least, theoretically — the denominations at work within these areas. Young people's committees within the states, counties and communities bear responsibility for the coöperative work in these areas. In addition, there is a growing development of young people's councils, made up of young people and adults, within communities, districts, counties, and states. They give promise of becoming an effective means of coöperative Christian activity.

" The council membership should be as representative as possible. The plan in most common use is to have four young people (two boys and two girls) and one adult leader from each local church, elected officially by the local church, as members of the council. These delegates are usually elected by the young people themselves and approved by the official board of the church. There are some cases where six young people are permitted from each church, having two delegates from the young people's societies. There are also a few cases where the Y.M.C.A., the Y.W.C.A., and the public school are represented."[1]

This plan of coöperation has received the official endorsement of the denominations through the International Council. The churches, therefore, are at the point where they will be invited to share in this organizational development.

The council should provide a means by which an exchange of plans and methods may become available to all groups. "Another program" should not be mediated to the local churches. Rather, all useful suggestions issued by any agency are to be offered to local groups as aids in the construction of their curriculum. One of the chief aims should be to strengthen church school classes and departments by acquainting them with what their denominational leaders have to offer and by giving them an opportunity, also, to know what is going on in the general field of young people's work. In addition, large coöperative ventures should be undertaken in the name of all the churches.

The council should think in terms of the total young people's program. A present danger is that councils will become competing union agencies; the same young people will be appealed to by the council, the Christian Associations and the Christian Endeavor Union. It will be a mistaken policy if the council is established either in the hope of killing or crippling existing coöperative bodies, or of ignoring them. There should be an effort

[1] From "*Youth in Coöperation*" (Christian Quest pamphlet) p. 15. Copyright, International Council of Religious Education. Used by permission.

to find a way of linking the activities of this organization with similar inter-church agencies.

d. Federations or councils of churches. As in the national field the Federal Council of Churches has had a Commission on Education, so in many communities where federations of churches exist, there is a department or committee which deals with religious education. There is merit, from the standpoint of abstract logic, in the suggestion that the national program of religious education should be a part of the work of the Federal Council, for if the Federal Council is the churches at work together, and if religious education is a phase of church activity, then the national program of religious education should be carried on through the agency which represents the united church in its total program. But whether this abstract logic applies, depends upon human and realistic considerations.

The problem as it applies in the local field is the same: Is not the federation of churches the means through which the young people's council and similar religious education agencies can best work? Where this issue comes up the whole matter should be faced with open minds, with a fair consideration of the existing agencies and of the various possibilities. Certainly no federation is justified in setting up a rival council or a competing organization of young people or a new program for the churches where an approved interdenominational agency already exists, unless that body has become ineffective.

Some of the best city-wide interdenominational work in America has had its origin in the federations of churches. The general principles which prevail in organizing committees or councils, directly related to the state councils of religious education, should be observed when the church federation is the supervising agency. The governing boards should be composed of the official denominational educational leaders, together with other experts in this field. The programs promulgated should be the individual plans of the communions together with the joint programs agreed upon by all of them together.

In the field of interdenominationalism there is as much danger of competition as among the denominations themselves. We need a correlation of interchurch bodies almost as badly as we do of denominations. A general warning needs to be sounded to all coöperative agencies: that they play fair with the organizations which were on the field before they came into being, that they specialize in those ranges of church work where nothing significant is yet being done; that they be cautious not to multiply problems, rather than to simplify them, by creating another means of propagandizing (if not exploiting) the young people of the churches and their adult leaders. Certainly it should be possible where councils of religious education and federations of churches exist to establish a fine working relationship between the two. A satisfactory solution would be to have the council recognized as the education commission of the federation.

Coöperation in Program

In many communities the matter of actual affiliation with the several agencies of interchurch coöperation is not a burning question. Where this is true, there should be no undue eagerness to approach this phase of the problem. The approach, rather, should be through coöperation in activities. The forming of a paper organization does not make interdenominationalism. Agreement and participation in the promotion of common interests will eventually create the attitude of mind which will produce an organizational unity. There are, in almost every community, many things which can better be done together than separately. Either through a permanent organization or through temporary committees the leaders in the local churches will do well to plan, each year, for a number of union activities.[2] After a period of such combined

[2] A list of activities suitable for common effort is given in Appendix IV.

effort, church divisions will become less distinct, the likenesses between Christians will appear greater than their differences, and the ground work will be laid for that church union which will come with the years. Coöperation in program activities is a much more pressing need, in most neighborhoods, than is the formation of any type of interchurch organization.

Materials Recommended for Further Study

Athearn, Clarence R. *Interchurch Government.* Century.

Athearn, Walter S. *A National System of Education.* Doubleday, Doran.

Butterfield, Kenyon L. *A Christian Program for the Rural Community.* Cokesbury Press.

Fiske, George W. *Community Forces for Religious Education.* Cokesbury Press.

Harper, William A. *An Integrated Program of Religious Education.* Macmillan.

Hooker, Elizabeth R. *United Churches.* Doubleday, Doran.

Richardson, Norman E. and Loomis, Ormand E. *The Boy Scout Movement Applied by the Church.* Scribner's.

Steiner, Jesse F. *Community Organization.* Century.

Van Kirk, Walter W. *Youth and Christian Unity.* Doubleday, Doran.

Youth and Cooperation. International Council of Religious Education. (Christian Quest booklet.)

Chapter XI

THE PASTOR AND HIS YOUNG PEOPLE

THE minister is the key-man in young people's work. His personal attitude and interest count more than that of any two or three adults. He is to the young people the living symbol of the church. Their criticism of organized religion or their deep affection for the Christian church depends as much upon the character and the spirit of the pastor as upon any other single factor. His ability to enter into their experiences or his failure to understand their ideas is interpreted as representing the "old folks" generally. Young people will overlook a good deal of adult neglect if their pastor is for them; they will forget many of their elders' efforts in their behalf if the minister is too busy to help them with their program and their problems.

Boys and girls expect their pastor to reveal the noble and desirable elements of personal character. They do not admire a man who makes concessions in the realm of principles or morality. Flippancy is no more honored than funereal self-righteousness. They want a minister to be one of them in the spirit of social fellowship, but they do not demand that a mature person shall try to act the part of an adolescent. Reality is essential to them. They will overlook defects, but they insist upon genuine Christian virtues and a sympathetic disposition toward their present interests. They cannot endure a prying or hypercritical attitude, but they want frankness and honesty from a pastor whom they trust because they have been convinced that he trusts and honors them. Other adults can be of great assistance. A pastor's wife can make up for some of the minister's limitations (for no man is equally capable in all respects), church school teachers can compensate for some of his busyness, but the minister continues to be the living interpretation of the spirit of the church. Many shortcomings of the adult membership will be condoned if the pastor is a genuine Christian friend. He stays in the center of youth's mental image of the church. He is, for them, the incarnation of present-day Christianity. Youthful habits and ideas are being determined by the entire adult environment, but the minister has the opportunity of giving the church a reputation much higher than the actual present life of the church warrants. He can help young people to understand that Christianity is not to be thought of entirely on the basis of the average level which Christian civilization has so far reached, but in terms of individual achievement and of ideals made real in an occasional life. If a pastor wants young people to develop a loyalty to the church he must maintain a live and nonprofessional interest in them, individually and collectively, an interest which is buttressed by a genuinely Christian experience and a loyal discipleship to Jesus Christ.

He is the key-leader from an official standpoint also. He alone does not determine the policies of the church, but he must formulate many of them, and he is its leader. If the young people are to have a fair chance for free life within the institution, it will be because he takes the initiative in providing an adequate leadership and support. If religious education is ever to gain the full recognition in the church's program which it deserves, it will be because the pastor intelligently and enthusiastically interprets its fundamental significance for the future of the race. If the old-fashioned Sunday school is to make way for a modern program — pedagogically sound and extending throughout the week — the transformation will not come about without much serious planning and a great deal of convincing argument and sacrificial labor. Usually, the pastor must take the initiative. If others lead, he must at least give constant and informed support. If a competent corps of teachers is to be secured, it will be because the minister has magnified the possibilities open to leaders of youth, and has placed the responsibility at the door of men and women best fitted, in character and potentiality, to undertake the service. A minister's interest in religious education as a means of growing Christian life may be judged by the frequency with which his sermons recur to the elements of the process of Christian nurture — a process which is continuously going on in the home, on the playground, at school, in the church, and in higher educational institutions. Even when a director of religious education is specifically charged with the development and administration of the church-school program, the whole enterprise will succeed or fail to the degree that interested and intelligent church support has been stimulated through the minister's active leadership.

Just as the manager of a corporation must be conversant with the policies of all department heads, and must give earnest commendation to such as are acceptable and must coöperate in improving such plans as seem to be out of line with the organization's general purposes, so the pastor cannot resign all responsibility for young people's work just because professional assistance has been secured for the church school. He will not, of course, obtrude to the disadvantage of the educational expert. He will do nothing which will make more difficult or less conspicuous the unique contribution which the director of religious education has to offer. He will reënforce that work at every point. But in order to do that he must be conversant both with the developments within the field of religious education generally and with the specific intentions of the local director. The effectiveness of the program of the minister of education is assured only when the pastor gives it his loyal support, a support which will win the practical approval of parents and young people. It is surprising how far a reactionary superintendent or a doubting church board can be brought if the expert's opinions are corroborated by the sober and studied judgment of a sane minister, a minister whose ability to "see things whole" is relied upon by his laymen.

His Personal Attitude and Equipment

1. Sympathy with young life. In order to maintain an understanding attitude toward youth it is not necessary for an adult to approve the drift of present-day morality or the vagaries of current thought. The persons who are most effective as advisors and as agents of conversion are those who understand the pulls and passions of the inner man, and who realize the seeming helplessness of the individual in the midst of social forces. It is necessary not only to appraise the moral status of modern youth but to understand also why they are what they are. Adults, generally, are too eager to criticize and too disinclined to watch calmly the forms of youthful self-expression. Partly because the pastor stands as the representative of a gospel which is dissatisfied with half-goodness, and also because tradition and fictional representations have pictured the clergyman as a not-of-this-world being, young people are suspicious if not fearful of the minister. They expect to be frowned upon, to be "called down," for their ideas and social practices. This is unfortunate, for the reputation does not correspond to the disposition of most ministers; but the suspicion exists, and the pastor must overcome it through personal interest and a genuine good fellowship.

2. **Pastoral opportunity.** It is generally agreed that one of the most useful contributions of the university pastor is his ability to "get next to students" and to advise them in their personal perplexities — worries that range all the way from the formulation of a life philosophy to the solution of a love complication. These students who come in confidence to these father confessors usually find it a new and satisfying experience, one which was unknown to them during high-school days in their home churches. Not

every high-school student is bursting with problems which he wants to confide to some adult, but hosts of them are longing for the opportunity of unburdening their hearts. This is attested by the universal summer conference experience with high-school delegates. They disclose the inner secrets and desires and problems of their hearts in perfect frankness to a stranger — a stranger who has shown by his manner that he understands them and that he has an experience which may be of help to them. Why did they not do it at home, to their parent, their teacher, their pastor? It is rare today, tragically rare, for young people to approach their parents with these secrets. The church-school teacher has not usually become this confidante. Nor has the pastor. Who is to blame? None of us adults desire this embarrassment on the part of youth, and yet we have created it — by our busyness, our aloofness, our professionalism, our fixity of opinion, our inability actually to live with young people.

The adult, whose relation to young people is primarily professional and formal, seldom penetrates to the secret places of the heart. The pastor who chums with young people, individually and in groups, as much because it renews his own youth and gives buoyancy to his spirit as because he thinks of them as parishioners, will render a cumulative service of inestimable significance. He does not need to be a "good fellow" in the sense of sacrificing study for play. The "good sport" idea can be carried too far; its value is overrated. If a minister plays tennis because he likes to, the court is one of the finest places for companionship with young people. If he enjoys riding or hiking, it is a natural and profitable practice to pick up a fellow or two. But it is absurd to think that the only natural method of making contacts with young people is through play. It is just as logical to do it through work undertaken together. Many a middle-aged pastor, who understands youth, has far greater success than young men just out of the seminary who depend so largely upon sports to make their point of contact. The main consideration is that the adult leader, who typifies the church, shall be able to associate gladly and naturally with the growing generation, speaking words of praise when honors are won, calling upon them in sickness, seizing every opportunity for worthwhile conversation, and making himself available for conference at any time.

The pastor should seek to make himself useful in helping young people to face four of the major decisions of life. The church-school teacher will be of assistance in these same matters, but the pastor must furnish a certain amount of background information and of inspiration through the service of worship, and he may seize many opportunities of helping the young people along these lines: (a) decision to make Jesus the guide for personal living; (b) decision to join the church; (c) choice of a life work; (d) choice of a life partner. The pastor will usually take the initiative in inviting young people to join the church. In many cases this is done through one or two classes each year, and the Lenten period has come to be a common time for the pastoral class by which young people are prepared for an intelligent affiliation with the church. These general problems, together with the multitude of specific issues related to them, are being met by ministers in various ways: (a) a series of sermons or talks in the regular church service or at designated sessions of the school; (b) a systematized plan of regular pastoral attention, with a confidential record of needs and interests; (c) little group meetings in the pastor's study of four or five young people who are thinking seriously along some special line; (d) the leadership of a church-school class for a given period while these themes are uppermost by arrangement with the superintendent and teacher; (e) question-boxes in connection with the school or society.

3. A sense of values. It is foolish to say: "The church might as well forget the old folks; you can't do anything with them, anyhow. You might better devote all of your effort to the young people." One of the difficulties today, where progressive work is under way among young people, is that older people who have not kept abreast of modern educational developments are a heavy handicap. The whole church must move apace. Adult education is one of the main responsibilities which the minister bears. Without neglecting the slow and difficult task of adult instruction and evangelization, the pastor must give such time and thought to the adolescent age range as it deserves. He must see the two phases of his work as parts of a single whole. He cannot neglect the one without serious consequences to the total program. He must regard an appointment with a high-school junior as just as important as an engagement with the president of the bank. He must be present at scheduled meetings where he is expected in the case of young people as certainly as at the trustees' meeting. Young people must be granted the use of the church building ungrudgingly. They must be in the affectionate thought of the pastor as are his own children in his family life. If adolescents are to receive their share of attention and be given their full portion of the responsibility in the total church program it will be because the minister thinks of young people's work as a rich opportunity and not as just "another burden."

4. **A knowledge of religious education.** This department of study was not included in the seminary curriculum when our middle-aged pastors graduated. They, therefore, must educate themselves in this field of activity, through the reading of books, conferences with workers at institutes, and a practical acquaintance with problems and methods. The fact is that a good many ministers who have never had any specialized training in the subject have become the most successful workers with young people, and on an educational plane. It is a tragedy that many ministers coming from some theological seminaries today are wholly unequipped for young people's work in the churches. This is not, of course, universally true. A few schools are rendering the

double service: (a) providing a sure philosophical and pedagogical foundation, and (b) introducing the students to the variety of types of situations which they are likely to face when they go to their first parishes and providing them with constructive suggestions by which they may work their way through such situations.

Usually the pastor is better equipped mentally and educationally than the average member of his teaching force. If the level of the church-school work is to be high, it will be because he lifts it. The minister cannot afford to be in the position of trying to " catch on " to what his teachers learned at a leadership training school. There is no reason for pride in asserting, " I don't know what this is all about. I'm old-fashioned and cannot keep up with these new-fangled developments." A minister dare not pass by the best new book on religious education any more than he can ignore the theological " book of the year." It is a part of his duty to read the standard religious education periodicals as thoroughly as he does the missionary journals. If there are training institutes at which technical information is to be made available, he must furnish the urge which will send his teachers; and he should not think himself above registering for such courses.

5. Interpreting the generations. The most common plaint of young people is " My parents don't understand me." A frequent cry of despair from fathers and mothers is " I can't figure this younger generation out." Both statements are true. Neither needs to be true. Neither adults nor young people have usually made an earnest and open-minded and unselfish effort to get the other's viewpoint.

Because the church embraces all ages and succeeds only as it ministers to the needs of all and as all dwell together in unity as members of a true family of Christ, one of the minister's continuing opportunities is that of interpreting young and old to each other and of leading them to a proud and joyful sense of unity in fellowship. This is not easy. There are no patented methods of accomplishing it. The sermons, however, will show it if the pastor has a clear understanding of the foibles and fidelities of both generations. A church night which is planned in the interest of all, and with specific provision for the varied groups, will go a long way toward accentuating the family idea. Committee meetings will demonstrate the desire of all to consider all, with all ages regularly represented on these committees. The social and financial programs of the church will bear witness to the deep desire of all to make the church a truly coöperative institution. The pastor will understand old and young better than they understand themselves, and will slowly bring the whole group to an appreciation of the unique requirements of the several age-groups and of the common interests and needs of all.

6. Living a life. The movie representation of the parson disgusts us all. The modern "go-getting" efficiency expert is likely not to be permanently popular or fundamentally helpful. Young people, like business men, prefer a minister who is able to "mix well." But that is not their most insistent demand. They want him to be more human than professional, more Christian than cleric or efficiency engineer. Our religion is incarnate if it lives at all. The great gulf which exists between knowledge of the right and actual righteous conduct will probably be bridged only as we successfully appeal to the affectional side of a person. This affection may be an attachment to an ideal, but usually it is an ideal made real in human flesh. Our hope is that growing youth will see Jesus as this incarnated ideal, and it is true that they come to Jesus more easily if they find in his disciples in present society that which commends him to them. Young people expect Christianity to be clearly apparent in the leader of the Christian forces. When they find it in their minister there is great likelihood that they will develop those life loyalties which they believe this pastor possesses. It is not a different demand that young people make than that which church members generally should insist upon: that the Christian minister first reveal God and Jesus and the way of Christ-like life. This is the part of the program which will go deepest. It is the phase of the leader's influence which will last longest. The radiation of a religious life is the main method of religious education.

The Sunday "Church Service"

The general worship services of the church constitute an important phase of the religious education program. It has been argued that the morning service cannot be both a worship occasion and an instructional opportunity; that consequently the pastor must make a choice as to whether this shall produce the satisfaction which comes from "enjoying God" or whether it shall be didactic in character. As is apparent from the preceding chapters of this book, religious education is not confined to instruction and is not opposed to worship, which is a part of the educational process just as it is a central element in religion. Whether the Sunday service be largely liturgical or almost completely instructional, it constitutes a significant educational factor. If young people attend it with awe or satisfaction, or come away with a sense of challenge, the single experience cannot help affecting their lives. The experience frequently or regularly repeated becomes a moving force within them. Of course, the church fails in making the educational process complete unless it also offers chances by which this good intention and impulse may be transformed into social character. If young people, on the other hand, attend the service once or repeatedly, with a lack of understanding, with an experience of dissatisfaction, without any sharpened ambition for worthwhile living, the service provides an education which is opposed to its religious intention. The pastor is perhaps the chief agent of religious education in the church; his Sunday church service is a medium through which he adds " line upon line " and determines thinking and emotional response and attitudes and life directions. This is true for young people, too, and the effect of the general church services upon their appreciation of religion is much greater than church-school leaders have thus far recognized.

The criticism is frequently made, both by those who are thoughtful and by many who are more critical than erudite, that they " don't get anything out of the church service." The best attitude to take toward such a criticism is that of self-examination. All of us find ourselves running into certain habits which sometimes become ruts. It may be that our church service has moved, unconsciously, in a direction in which young life cannot easily follow. Have we thought about young people as we have prepared the sermon? Just what was there in today's service which would make a special appeal to the understanding of youth? The service should not become puerile or sensational; but in its arrangement, as in its thought, young people's abilities and needs should be considered along with those of their parents.

But this in itself is not enough to lead all young people to a full appreciation of the possible fruitage of Sunday worship. As has already been suggested in chapter VI, it is important that a formal or informal process of instruction shall enable the growing generation to understand the values which are inherent in corporate worship, so that there may be a gradually greater appreciation of their significance.

It is not a simple matter to cultivate and maintain the habit of church-going upon the part of young people today, if we are placing emphasis upon the church-school class and the evening society. Adults should face the problem of how many meetings it is fair to expect young people to attend on Sunday. Which of the several sessions has the largest value for them? After such a study has been made, every effort should be expended in making the church meetings so attractive that interest will compel loyalty. The adults in the home have a heavy responsibility in providing the right encouragement to young people to be faithful to church duties, a responsibility which will not be met by nagging or critical urging, and which cannot be secured unless the family life has so been lived that young people see the value of church attendance and have a loving respect for the desires of their parents. Unless parents themselves show a fidelity in church attendance, a fidelity which grows out of appreciation and results in appreciation rather than a scornful criticism of preacher and service, it can hardly be expected that young people will go to church in that spirit which will provide a wholesome religious education.

1. Appreciate the importance of developing a loyalty to the church service. When high-school graduates go away to college or to a job in another community, most of them will not continue to attend the classes of the church school. This may be unfortunate, but it is a fact which it does no good to dodge. Many of them will not attend the evening discussion group, unless they fall in with some one who introduces them to this program. If they continue their loyalty to a church, the likelihood is that they will join the adults at "church service." It will be very easy not to do this. It is such a temptation to lie in bed late, to read and write and work and go somewhere with the crowd. Only a loyalty to the church, established during younger years and reënforced by an experience of the worthwhileness of attendance, will carry them through these days of their new freedom. Because this is true, it is very important that during the intermediate and senior years, the pastor and parents should coöperate in making the morning church service of great value to young people. We do not want our young people to graduate from the church school, but if it becomes a choice between the class and morning worship when they have reached the senior years of high school, there is something to be said in favor of the church service, provided that service has real help in it for them.

2. **Consider young people an important part of the congregation.** The preacher must think in terms of the young as well as of the old in his announcement of sermon subjects and the preparation of the sermon content. No campaign for the attendance of adolescents will amount to much until the church has established an attitude and a practice which will assist the growth of youthful interest. As he prepares his sermon, every minister probably visualizes some of the persons who sit in the congregation. There are Deacon Brown and Mrs. Merriweather and Professor Atkins. But does he also see John Jones? Will John understand what he is talking about? Is he preaching in polysyllables with the professor in mind? Are those theological terms particularly for the benefit of the deacon? Not in any bad sense would a Christian minister mould his message to please or attract individuals. And yet, in checking on himself, he frequently finds that the opinions of these persons have more to do with the sermon than he wishes were the case. Then, of course, Professor Atkins needs a particular message; he is a good man but he has certain lopsided notions which need straightening out. And Mrs. Merriweather is a woman of ability who loves the church; but she is giving more time to club work and less to the church, and this message should strike her conscience. And the deacon is a noble Christian, but he has not kept abreast of the times, and one of the minister's tasks is to make religion a more present reality for him.

But what about John Jones? What change needs to be made in the sermon for him? It will not be necessary to dilute the message; it may be necessary to simplify it or to couch it in terms which correspond with his present experience. There will need to be a certain concreteness which finds illustration in the realm of young life as well as in adulthood. This concreteness must ally itself with the fundamental principles about which both young and old need to be brought to think, and to which they need to give a fresh loyalty. It will be discovered that what has meaning for John has equal meaning for the deacon and the professor and Mrs. Merriweather. This will not be talking down to youth; it will merely be a recognition that they are there — or ought to be. Such an ability to include young people within the range of the sermon thought and yet not to single them out for extended special treatment, and also to lift their minds to truths which they cannot yet fully comprehend but about which they should be thinking, will be in no small measure a result of the pastor's constant contacts with young life. The prayer, which ought to be the fruit of brooding and deep thought and love, should envisage the range of adolescent problems and experiences, and should be so constructed as to lead the thoughtful participation of young people. Frequently, the greatest service which an hour of worship can render is offered in the pastoral prayer.

3. **Give them responsibility for the service.** It is a wholesome practice to have young men serve along with their elders as ushers for the church. There is more value than we know (for the congregation as well as for the participants), in having boys take up the offering. One of the most lasting influences has resulted from choirs made up of young people. A group of university workers, discussing the equipment with which freshmen come to college, agreed that the most that the church had done was to develop a certain kind of loyalty as a result of choir singing. There is even more value in appointing junior deacons to serve with older men, and in placing young people on every important committee of the church. Frequently, in our smaller churches particularly, the evening service is a combination of the young people's meeting and the general worship. Young people share in the pulpit responsibility at some of the evening meet-

ings; probably more young people have had their interest turned to full-time Christian service because of such experiences than by any other single method of church work.

The Church School and Class

There are no fixed rules which can determine the individual pastor's duty with reference to organizations for young people. How much he must do depends upon the amount of leadership available in the parish, the variety of other tasks for which he himself must feel personal responsibility, the kind of thing which he can do best, and upon countless other factors in the local situation which no one can analyze except by a careful study of the particular church. A pastor, faithful to the whole parish responsibility and eager to make his ministry among young people count in the largest possible way, will find that policy which seems wisest for his own field. The following questions are some of the many which most ministers have to face and think through.

1. **Should the pastor superintend the church school or a department?** Generally, the answer would be in the negative. This is a task for which some layman should be prepared. Moreover, if the minister is to assume a regular weekly charge in the young people's division, it is probably better for him to be a teacher than to administer a department. There are, however, exceptions, as when the minister assumes the position temporarily in order to demonstrate a policy which he believes should prevail, or to fill in during a period when a layman is being equipped to undertake the work.

2. **Should he teach a class?** This, too, will be answered in the negative by many ministers who feel that they have too many duties without taking on this large assignment. Sometimes, however, the pastor is exactly the man to lead a group of boys. If he is, and if it is certain that no one else can have quite the same constructive influence upon them that the minister can, he should

take the group, making such adjustments in his schedule as will enable him to give conscientious attention to the whole program of the class. No minister should accept such an opportunity unless he is willing and able and determined to spend a great deal of time with the boys. It will not only be bad for the young people, if he "soldiers on the job," but will react unfavorably upon the minister and upon the entire church. Pastors who do not accept a regular teaching assignment may find that there are certain occasions during the year when issues are raised regarding which it seems the pastor has a greater competence for leadership than any other adult.

3. Should he be the counselor for the evening group? It should not be taken for granted that he is the counselor; if the group wants him to act in such a capacity, it is well for him to accept. But he must recognize that he is entering upon an obligation which demands time, requires tact and breadth of mind, and involves him in a good deal more than merely attending a meeting each week. Usually, it is better to have some lay leader in the position of counselor, if the right person is available and is acceptable to the church committee and to the young people. The pastor can function as an unofficial advisor, provided he does not do it officiously and does not try to spoil or discount the plans which have been developed coöperatively by the executive committee and the approved counselor. When issues arise which seem to demand some attention from the general leader of the church, the approach should be quietly made to the officers of the group, in the spirit of conference rather than with the authority of a pronouncement handed down from above.

4. Should he attend the sessions of the school and society? Usually, he should. This is one way of showing an interest in the work and of developing an appreciation of the significance of the program. If the society should feel, however, that it cannot express itself so completely when he is present, the pastor will do well to absent himself temporarily and gracefully, using such opportunities as he can find to make himself a warm friend of the members, coming in occasionally, showing that sympathetic and understanding spirit which will impress the young people with his sincere friendliness and great worth as an advisor. Almost certainly, he will be invited to come regularly. If he is a regular attendant, he should not take any conspicuous part in the meetings, unless he is asked to do it. There are times when he will want to talk, and fewer times when he really ought to talk. He must control himself, trusting the young people to see themselves through a discussion, preferring to add his counsel at the close of the meeting rather than inserting it at many points in the discussion, unless it has been agreed that he is to keep the discussion to the point as it goes along. Discussions need just this guidance; but if the pastor is to undertake this duty, as he probably is equipped to do, the initiative should come from the young people. Even then, he should constantly be checking himself so that he will not do all the talking or thinking for the group. It is a dangerous thing for young people to get the idea that he is there primarily as policeman; if there is disorder, he must find some other way of helping to solve the problem than by scolding or referring to it frequently in the meetings.

5. How far should he push himself forward in young people's work? The best attitude is that of making it understood that he is always available for any kind of help in the morning and evening and midweek activities of the division and society, but that he does not expect to thrust himself forward into the activities of these organizations, for the leadership of which properly appointed or elected officials are responsible. It is a good thing for young people to come to their pastor and ask for definite help; this is better than to have it constantly wished upon them. At the same time, the minister will need to be careful not to give the impression that he is so completely absorbed elsewhere that he cannot give much time or thought to young people. Whether or not it be thought the prerogative of the minister to keep his hands on all the lines of the church's activity, with full authority to change policies when his judgment dictates, it is unwise for him to stand upon his rights except in very grave situations. Young people's work must be conducted in a democratic and not a paternalistic fashion. The educational process rather than the assertiveness of authoritarianism must prevail. A sense of humor serves the pastor in good stead in his dealing with youth. He, along with other adults, must sometimes be willing to be in the background of the picture. Young people are very susceptible to suggestion and advice; they always say that what they will do with it depends upon "who gives it and the manner in which it is given."

Materials Recommended for Further Study

The materials here listed are of the type which will help the pastor to think through the problems which interest young people. They do not deal with the method by which the minister can increase his effectiveness with young people; there is little of value printed on that subject, except as the materials referred to at the end of the fifth chapter are as useful for him as for teachers in the church school.

Barbour, Dorothy D. *Making the Bible Desired.* Doubleday, Doran.

Belden, Albert D. *The Religious Difficulties of Youth.* Cokesbury Press.

Boorman, William R., and others. *Jesus and a Boy's Philosophy of Life.* Association Press.

Brown, Charles R. *Why I Believe in Religion.* Macmillan.

Brown, William A. *Beliefs That Matter.* Scribner's.

Davis, Ozora S. *The Credentials of the Church.* Macmillan.

Eddy, Sherwood. *Sex and Youth.* Doubleday, Doran.

Eiselen, Frederick C., and others. *Christianity Today.* Cokesbury Press.

Fosdick, Harry E. *Twelve Tests of Character.* Association Press.
Grenfell, Wilfred T. *What the Church Means to Me.* Pilgrim Press.
Mather, Kirtley. *Science in Search of God.* Holt.
Royden, A. Maude. *I Believe in God.* Harpers.
Streeter, B. H. *Moral Adventure.* Macmillan.
Swain, Richard L. *What and Where Is God?* Macmillan.

CHAPTER XII

THE TWO GENERATIONS

THE church is a family of families. It is not the unique possession of any generation. It has its foundations in the past, it builds for the future. Its constituency includes the very youngest and the most aged. It must use all who can make any contribution to its welfare and to its world-wide task. It must strive to meet the life needs of children and young people and middle-aged and the very old. No single group within the church must complain because the pastor and the voluntary leadership give thought and time and spend money to guide, strengthen, or comfort any other age level of the membership. The young sometimes are jealous of the attention given to the aged. They have not considered the wide responsibility of this family institution, nor have they had the experience to appreciate the unique requirements of those of mature years. The middle-aged are sometimes critical of the adaptations of program which are made to satisfy and help adolescents; they have become old-fashioned in their viewpoints and have lost the ability to think in youthful terms. But, despite these failures on the part of all to see things whole, the church continues to try to meet its obligation: a genuine ministry to all of human life. Our fault is not so much in our intention as in our understanding. The two generations need to look sympathetically at each other and then to join in a satisfying fellowship based on deep affection. The guiding ideas for such a family relationship may be found in the thirteenth chapter of First Corinthians. This final discussion attempts to interpret to both generations some of the existent attitudes within the church, in the hope that, separately and together, young and old may appraise their own situation, may make such changes in their group life as will create a genuinely Christian relationship within the church-family, and may thereby contribute to the establishment of the Kingdom of God throughout the world by a demonstration of what it is like in the smaller primary units of society: the home and the church and the community.

a – THE CHURCH ATTITUDE TOWARD YOUTH

Viewed from an adult standpoint, what is the task of the church regarding its youth? At least four ideas of the task of the church persist in our thinking and practice.

1. To save our young people. The doctrine of salvation is one of the cardinal ideas of the church. During most of Christian history it was thought of largely in terms of the individual, and the common idea was that its chief aim was to save the individual from eternal punishment. In more recent days, the emphasis has been upon the fact that Christianity saves a man from his evil impulses and redeems him to a wholesome rounded life which brings that abundance of experience regarding which Jesus spoke. But this idea has not come into the consciousness of young people, generally, and the very word " salvation " connotes to them that mysterious and somewhat questionable transformation which is associated with golden streets and a quenchless flame.

The doctrine of salvation rests upon the continuing experience of the power of religion. If Christianity has a unique task it is to provide the power by which we are able to do those things which our intelligence tells us we should do, and to restrain us from that life which we know is sin. Young people in all times need to be saved from themselves and from the sins of social life. In every generation they will need to be saved to that type of character which was manifest in Jesus and which is the revelation of God himself.

But the method which accompanies the theology of salvation is usually psychologically unsound and dangerous. When young people have the idea that the church exists to save them, they react as most of us do against the thought of the tabernacle revival. Boys and girls resent the idea that they are "lost," that they must be saved. They know that they are not perfect, they are often aware of their sins and worry more about them than their parents do; but they know also that they are not completely bad and that any rational viewpoint cannot call them lost. Moreover, they doubt very much whether the church has a salvation to offer that can make them entirely new creatures. They sometimes hint that those adults who are most anxious to communicate a salvation have enough to do to appropriate that salvation themselves. They recognize that what one does not have in ample measure he cannot pass on to others.

The need of a higher type of living is apparent to youth; they understand that adults can be of great help. But the superiority involved in the thought of the adult church as a saving agency repels the younger generation, and the method associated with the theology arouses resentment. We need a new terminology, with a corresponding change in attitude on the part of adults, and an educational method which will slowly and surely accomplish that saving result which the old paternalism and the catastrophic theology did not achieve. For our youth need to be kept from the common sins of the ages and from the intellectual and emotional and physical sins which have such unique expressions today. The church should be equipped, from the standpoint of exemplary adult counselors and of scientific educational procedure to help these young people to keep themselves from sin and to dedicate themselves to righteousness. Only as they lay hold of the power which comes from God, communicated to most of us through personal attachment to and powerful affection for Jesus, can such sins be overcome and such triumphant living be achieved. But this cannot be accomplished with any assurance of success if the attitude of adulthood is that of the teacher who says "Now, young man, I'm going to make you good."

2. **To serve the young people.** Out of a genuine love for young life has grown an adult eagerness to place the fruits of experience on the laps of the growing generation, and to make the church an effective instrument for the service of boys and girls. There is an increased willingness to provide social rooms for adolescents, to give them such use of the church property as they desire, to overlook the occasional damage to chairs and windows, to prepare and serve suppers for their frequent gatherings and to wash the dishes after the young people have had their fun, to give themselves in thoughtful service as teachers or counselors even though this may mean the sacrifice of cherished personal pleasures. "Young people must be served" has been the dominating idea.

This is a hopeful advance over the doctrine of rescue. It is the extension of the sacrificial spirit of the mother into the realm of community and church life. It has a relation to Jesus' emphasis upon ministry as the duty of his disciples. It rests upon love and not upon fear. But there is a fundamental inadequacy about this attitude. It is not true, on the whole, that "young people must be served." Unfortunately there is a common impatience among them which demands that their meals be prepared when and in the way they want them, that their clothes shall be kept in shape for them, that all of the conveniences and many of the luxuries of life shall be provided whether the family budget can afford it or not. They are often thoughtless in small matters, they assume little or no responsibility for common home tasks, they allow a wearied mother to add to her labors those duties which they themselves ought to undertake voluntarily and faithfully.

But when it comes to the big matters, they feel themselves competent. They want to drive their own cars, buy their own clothes, handle their own (?) money, formulate their own philosophies, choose their own companions, determine their own life-work, dream their own dreams, make their own successes and mistakes.

They are accustomed at school to standing on their own feet. Much of the failure of church work is due to the fact that leaders have not recognized the potentialities of young people and their eagerness to do things for themselves — and for others, if this service is of their own choosing. Sound educational procedure will recognize the fact that the more young people plan and administer their own activities the greater their interest and the deeper their loyalty to the institution within which they work. The church will always need to serve youth, providing wise helpers, sound information, adequate equipment, and program assistance. But the attitude of adults must go beyond the "youth will be served" idea. An inevitable outcome of this attitude is the complaint, "They treat us like kids and don't think we know enough to run our own affairs."

3. **To use young people.** The women have the reputation of undertaking the really difficult tasks of the church. They have nourished and extended the missionary program when men would have let it dwindle and die. They have had the faith and energy and persistence to do the impossible in many a local situation. It was probably because of such enthusiasms that they first recognized the unlimited power that there is in young life. They were successful in mobilizing this power behind drives and campaigns. Individual churches have always given young people responsibilities. The national young people's societies have kept large service objectives before their membership, and for many years they held the enthusiasm of youth largely because of these activities. But so far as the denominational programs were concerned, the

women first allied the young people effectively behind extension plans and financial projects.

Benevolent boards have now accepted this method of engaging the interest of youth. Some of the denominational young people's programs are more promotional than educational, and are conceived largely with the thought that the active loyalty of boys and girls needs to be massed behind the denominational schemes. There is no disposition to deny the necessity of acquainting adolescents with what is being done by the church and what needs to be done, and of inviting their whole-hearted participation. But the idea of using young people is wrong, and consequently the approach is bad. The theory that representative officials of boards should lay out a world-wide program, and that young people should be expected to "get behind it," willy-nilly, is contrary to the psychology of youth and is a short-sighted policy. It rests upon an appeal to a presumed loyalty rather than involving a study of situations with a voluntary participation. It is not education so much as it is the propagandizing of institutional ideas and demands. It gives the young people the feeling that they are "being roped in"; it alienates the interest and often the presence of many of the most alert among the young; it creates the idea that "missions" is the equivalent of "begging for money"; it puts the church in the position of seeming to be an exploiter of youth.

We are fortunately moving rapidly away from this old method of appeal. From a merely utilitarian standpoint we recognize the danger of working a willing horse to death, or to rebellion. We see the defects of the attitude which says: "Now, Johnny, I want you to go shopping with me this afternoon instead of playing with the boys. I need you to carry the bundles." The usual response to a protest has been, "No arguing now. It is enough that mother wants you to do it. You must mind her." Johnny will go because he has to. He may even be convinced of the necessity of loyalty. But he does not understand the queer ways of parents. He stores up resentment. He is preparing himself for that rebellion and unleashed freedom which will come in later years. He is probably also in the way of becoming deceitful. This superior paternalism is not the way of the ideal family. No single group is to be considered the tool of another. Common and individual responsibility must be taught, but it cannot well be done in this fashion. Permanent and effective loyalty is secured through the coöperative process and not by edict or inveigling or imposition.

4. To share with youth the total life of the church. The fundamental difference between this new viewpoint and the traditional is that adults now include youth in their "we" and "our" and no longer think primarily in terms of "you" and "they." The peculiar interests and needs of various age levels continue to be recognized, just as individual differences are taken into account; but that deep and fearsome chasm which has yawned between the generations is closing. Life seems no longer a tug-of-war across the abyss. Each boy counts for one. An idea is an idea, regardless of the age of the mind in which it germinated. Personal responsibility is assumed by old and young alike because the entire group needs the best thinking and effort of all. Adult cynicism of youthful dreams is giving place to a proud delight in being included in the disclosures and hopes of adolescent minds. Youth's fear and mistrust of the suggestions of age are being displaced by eager interest and ready coöperation.

There is more of this new spirit than we sometimes realize. The adults of our churches have never been so anxious to take young people in as full-participating members. Their mistakes are due not so much to lack of right desire as to a fumbling inability to express themselves aright. They have lost the knack of living with young people. Our fast-moving social life has made calm and companionable family fellowship the exception.

But young people may be assured, bristling orators to the contrary, that never has there been so genuine a readiness as today on the part of the older generation to make it easy for adolescents to grow into full responsibility within the church. If youth will do its part to create the finer family atmosphere, there will usually be a response which is friendly and eager and open-minded.

Where pastors and adults still have a superiority complex, they had better set about earnestly to remove it. Where the idea prevails that the old folks know best what is right and that these young people will have their turn " when we are done," there had better be a revaluation of the purpose of the church. Is it the monopoly of a few elder statesmen or is it made up of those who love God and are seeking to serve him? How much do the elder statesmen love God if they make difficult a full sharing of the institution's life by those who are not so far removed as is the full-grown adult from the childlike spirit which must characterize the members of the kingdom of heaven? Does the older leader desire that the church shall live — live not for its own sake but to be a permanent light set on a height — and if he is thus anxious, how does he suppose that this institution which he now controls will live long beyond his own generation unless the youth of today develop a love and loyalty to it through an unrestrained co-operation in its tasks and benefits? The " hard-boiled " attitude which some stern elders still display is no different from that of melodrama; it is the shutting of the door of the home — only they do not own this house of God, even though they pay its bills! — in the face of the son who may have made a mistake, and who may still have more of the grace of God within him than the older church member. It is a heavy responsibility which adults within the church bear. Not so much by conscious disposition as by ingrained attitudes they sometimes stand between these young people and the Christ of God. Nothing less than a complete sharing of the life of the church by young and old will suffice. The gospel of Jesus is one of love and goodwill and respect for personality. It alone will bridge the chasms which divide our world. Where such chasms exist in the home or in the church, only the practice of the Christian gospel will bring peace and social health.

Youth's Attitude toward Religion and the Church

Just as there are various adult attitudes toward the growing generation and as the main trend seems to be toward a more complete understanding and a more friendly coöperation, so there is a variety of types of young people and the preponderating characteristics seem hopeful. Magazines and the daily press are full of discussions of this remarkable younger generation; the most conflicting statements have been made about them, and almost all are true — of some young people. Sour cynics have assured us that youth is headed for perdition, and self-appointed spokesmen have told us that if the world would but resign its leadership to young people, social salvation would be assured.

Most of the appraisals of adolescents have been in error at two points. In the first place, it has been assumed that young people are all alike. This is, of course, absurd. Twins, with a seemingly identical heritage and environment, may have few things in common except their looks and their age. Parents must treat them as individuals if peace and growth are to be assured. The church can never be very helpful to young people, nor can it incorporate them happily into its total life, until it recognizes that it must work with them on a personal as well as a mass basis. There is much opportunity for instruction and service through the class and department and society; but the greatest contribution which the church can make must rest upon a knowledge of individuals, personal friendliness and comradeship, the adaptation of program to personal requirements and capacities. The deeper things of life are not revealed in group meetings.

A second error common to the interpreters of modern youth is the notion that they are so different from the rest of humanity. They express themselves in weird ways, but these expressions represent the same desires and tendencies that move adulthood. Most of their ideas have their origin in adult minds; most of their practices ape what they have seen or heard among their elders. They follow the modes, in general, although they give occasional queer quirks to the prevailing styles. Many of their most monstrous ideas have been taken from books prepared by the middle-aged. Most of their highest ideals have been suggested by adults. Whether these young people follow the leadership of unbalanced popular stylists, or whether they copy the best which Christian character can reveal depends upon the quality and method of life in the home, among the neighbors on the street, in the church family, and in the community in which they live. Most of the criticism of youth must come back fundamentally to a condemnation of adult standards and practices. The generation which would cure the ills of growing youth cannot do it without first laying hold of social virtue itself.

It is impossible to classify accurately either the older or the younger generation. People are individuals. Still there are certain outstanding tendencies which make possible certain categories. With no scientific intent, but rather with the practical purpose of facing the church with certain distinct attitudes which prevail among our youth, the following attempt at interpretation is made.

1. The rebels. It is a commonly expressed belief that youth is "in revolt." There are certainly destructive tendencies in young life. Many seem occupied with the lawless business of throwing bricks through the windows; they gain a childish delight from breaking up the meeting. They pull at those pillars of civilization which have been erected through perspiring toil and at sacrificial pain. Nothing seems sacred: theologies, moralities, controls — these are in the discard. Within even the best of our young people there burn passions which threaten to destroy the soul. Moments of worship are succeeded by the wildest follies. Was there ever a time when it was not so?

This idea of the revolt of youth is overworked. A few startling instances outweigh the manifold evidences that purity and character have not departed from youth. Hosts of girls have character written in every feature, and boys innumerable have overcome temptations in a way that should put their parents to shame. But it is true that there are rebels. Some of them are outspoken critics of the church. Others " lambaste " the hypocrisies of our social system. A few insist that nationalism and patriotism are shibboleths which hide crime and dastardly conduct. Some announce that there are no eternal verities, that in the realm of morals the doctrine of relativity alone suffices. A few deny God. Hosts of them talk with brazen frankness regarding the personal intimacies of life — talk, often, with a sense of pleasure and out of an itching curiosity and not because they are deeply concerned with establishing goodness instead of badness and of building a new positive morality. A current tendency is toward complete anarchy in the moral realm. These facts are too apparent to be denied. Among those who share this tendency of the times are the sons and daughters from our best families, young people inside of the church as well as out.

What is the church's responsibility in such a day? First, it must take care not to give young people generally, and young people in particular, a reputation that they do not deserve. Where so much evil prevails it is easy to brand the whole company with the reputation which but a single member deserves-to exaggerate trivialities into grave sins. Gossip has wrought untold evil; it has made sinners of countless boys and girls whose motives were wholly virtuous. Adults must never give a boy the reputation of being a bad boy, or a girl the name of being a bad girl. Young people thus branded may well become ashamed of themselves and determine to live down the reputation. They may equally easily say, in effect, "I have the reputation and I might as well live up to it."

Positively, what can the church do? A first suggestion is that many of these rebels need a constructive task to challenge their energies. Boys who throw brickbats often find deep satisfaction in laying the foundation for a structure which will be a thing of beauty and of utility for the community. A second necessity is that the church shall face realities and be entirely willing to allow these revolters to express their exuberance or dissatisfaction within the church. It has been suggested in previous chapters that the church-school curriculum must take account of the issues which are at the root of present-day rebellion, that specific problems which are on the minds of youth should be openly and undogmatically considered, and that adult counselors themselves must not only understand but sympathize with the attitude of youth before they can be of great assistance in guiding them to a higher level of thought. And a third requirement is that the laxity which invites the criticism of youth shall be so corrected that the cause for complaint is removed, that the impulsive desires which move young people shall find control because they are faced with a quality of adult life which is its own commendation.

2. The idealists. There is nowhere in America so much idealism as is found among high school and college youth. Not all are dreamers; too few are. Not all want to establish a world-wide brotherhood; only a remnant are much concerned. But a larger per cent than one finds among the parents have visions of holy cities and of utopias. Therein lies great hope — and the despair of it all. The grave danger is that a young man will come home from college and announce with naïve enthusiasm to his father: "Dad, I have decided to make something of my life — not go in for money, you know, but make my life count for something. I'm thinking of the ministry or social service, or something like that." And then, with superior wisdom and feigned patience, the "hard-headed business man" replies: "Oh, that's all right, my boy. The dreams of youth — they won't hurt you. You'll come out all right. We all had our castles in the air. Just a few more years and you'll come down to earth. We live in a bread-and-butter world, you know. Well, what are the prospects for football for next fall?" How many a potential prophet has been made into a cynical practical man of affairs by this kind of scorn! And not uncommonly the father is a Sunday-school superintendent, a deacon, or a prominent supporter of the church (financially)! What does the church do to youthful idealists: harbor them, scorn them, thank God for them, put them in a prominent place of leadership? Unless our Christian society grows a crop of such idealists it is not much moved by the spirit of Jesus. If the church discourages this type of ebullient prophet, it will find itself in the position of being ignored or denounced by the greatest souls of the day, — Christian prophets who find their God more easily outside the church than in.

There are no genuine youth movements in America, so far as organized bodies are concerned. Many leaders claim such a designation for their organizations, others have tried to organize youth movements, but there is a surge within all of our Christian groups, which is the swelling power of youthful idealism. It is not by organization but by eager spirits within all organizations, that the forward movement of American Christianity must come. Several hundred thousand young people are in Christian conferences in the summer. Not all come home dreaming dreams, not all combine thoughtful resolution with fiery zeal. And yet these groups represent the idealistic leadership of our churches. If the home church will welcome their enthusiasm, will build upon their suggestions, will rally to their crusading spirit, there is nothing that cannot be accomplished by modern Christianity. If Christian youth do not take the leadership in cleaning up school politics, who will? If they do not stand united for a new morality based upon the fundamental verities found essential and satisfying by generations of earnest souls, who will? If Christian young people do not present to the community an incarnated Christ, a Christ through loyalty to whom they bridge the chasm between right intention and consistent action, who will? And if these idealisms and intentions are to be actualized, the church must move all its forces to make the questing and crusading spirit of the prophets of this new day easy and fruitful. The church comes upon a sad day when it discourages dreamers who know that they have an obligation to leave the world better than they found it. If new reformations are to come, much of the leadership will be found among the young.

3. **The drifters.** Those who constitute our major worry, among both the younger and the older generations, are that large mob who go wherever it seems easy and popular to go. They are not positively bad in the sense that they formulate fallacious philosophies or break down the cherished possessions of civilization; but if the crowd follows a fad, they are in the procession; if the mob surges against approved institutions, they move blindly along. These are the persons who follow the political dictation of party bosses or newspaper editors. They have learned, as Heywood Broun says, "to stand behind things but not to stand in front of anything." And because there are so many of them, the church and society face a permanent and baffling problem.

For such as these, the church must think its program through with care. Although it will not compete with the "world" it must develop a program which has interest as well as worth. The pastor must prepare his service for those who not only want meat but want it well flavored. The church school program must be so different that the mind-set against the "Sunday school" will be gradually overcome. It is not the first obligation of the church to become popular, but it has the duty of reaching the mass of men for their own sake. It is true of many of these drifters that they have eventually made the solid reliable stuff of which organized religion is constituted. A policy of patience, persistence, kindliness, and attractiveness is the only one which will gain the loyalty of the great mass of "giggling, gum-chewing youngsters who seem to have no purpose in life, and whose motto appears to be the old hymn, 'Oh, to be nothing!'"

4. The perplexed. It is probably a fact that most of the members of groups already discussed belong also in this last classification. Upon almost every subject, they have their earnest questions. Thomas Edison is a great specialist in his field, but the folly of dogmatism in an area outside one's realm of knowledge was revealed in an interview over the radio in which Mr. Edison was asked the question, "What advice would you give to young people?" With scornful certitude he replied, "There is no use giving young people advice; they won't take it." If one thing is true of youth generally, it is that their minds are popping with questions. They seem to be a perpetual interrogation point. That they won't always take advice is true, but that they will listen sympathetically is equally true. Whether they follow the counsel given them depends upon the character of the speaker, the amount of real information which he seems to have, the spirit in which he speaks to them — and then, the degree of intellectual and moral control that they have developed. The false assurance which often leads adults to say that "young people think they know it all; they're not willing to learn from anybody" is only a defense mechanism by which young people seek to protect themselves against that adulthood which thinks that all knowledge is wrapped up in itself.

The educational process, as has been indicated in other chapters of this book, must be one which makes questioning easy and natural and unrestrained. It must involve quest and experiment and vital activity. The curriculum must include those interests which occupy the minds of young people at the present moment. The church family must be of so friendly and congenial a temper that many of the questions of young minds will come to be answered by the fellowship of Christian souls, and many other questions will be naturally and frankly asked of those older persons whom their younger friends trust.

We are all members together of one body. If this body is to fulfill its complete function there must be healthy coöperation between the members. Paul's great words on this theme (Ephesians 4:11–16) apply to the need within our churches today. Looking at the whole adult-youth situation dispassionately, and with a sense of humor which at least equals our sense of tragedy, and observing the human stuff of which a community and a church are composed, young and old can make of their life together one joyful pursuit of high ideals and a coöperative achievement of social construction. Any such family fellowship will rest upon the recognition that there are faults in all, that goodness and kindliness and right intention are common possessions, that there is universal need for individual growth in character, and that new knowledge and great courage and an appropriation of the power of religion are prerequisites to any personal or social progress. With faces set to the future, forgetting the failures and inadequacies of Christians and Christian organizations in the past, Christians of this generation may appropriate the realism of the prophets, a realism which saw but did not condone the sins of the fathers or the devastations of their own time. But this realism must be combined with the prophetic idealism which knew that the kingdom of God could be established, and that it could be brought by earnest souls who labor together for its coming. Not forgetting that a Christian is his brother's keeper, old and young will succeed in making a Christian family of the church and of the community only as each person learns to keep his own household before he makes an assault upon the methods of his neighbor.

Laying hold of all the available science and pedagogy in an effort to give respectability to the church school and to enable it to do that for human life which will not need to be undone, the Christians of a community must yet understand that method and materials cannot do for boys and girls what personality can, and that religious education needs not so much to be standardized or codified as to be humanized. The aims of the program are to be conceived in terms of human need and potentiality. The main method is the multiform impact of personality on personality. The chief resource is human character, character which has been molded by the power of God into the likeness of Jesus Christ. The experience which we hope to help youth to achieve is that of a joyful and coöperative companionship with the Father. The divine soul has been revealed in divers ways — through nature and the printed page — but always the most effective medium for the complete revelation of the Heart of Love has been through his faithful children. It will always be so.

Materials Recommended for Further Study

Boorman, W. Ryland. *Developing Personality in Boys.* Macmillan.
Chesser, Elizabeth S. *Youth.* Dutton.
Coe, George A. *What Ails Our Youth?* Scribner's.
Cotton, Edward H. *Charles W. Eliot's Talks to Parents and Young People.* Beacon Press.
Edwards, R. H., J. M. Artman, and G. M. Fisher. *Undergraduates.* Doubleday, Doran.
Fiske, George W. *The Changing Family.* Harpers.
Harper, William A. *Youth and Truth.* Century.
Hollingworth, Leta A. *The Psychology of the Adolescent.* Appleton.
Hunter, Allan A. *Youth's Adventure.* Appleton.
Moxcey, Mary E. *The Psychology of Middle Adolescence.* Abingdon Press.

Mudge, E. Leigh. *The Psychology of Early Adolescence.* Abingdon Press.

——. *The Psychology of Later Adolescence.* Abingdon Press.

Overton, Grace S. *Youth in Quest.* Century.

Slattery, Margaret. *The Girl in Her Teens.* Pilgrim Press.

Stearns, Alfred E. *The Challenge of Youth.* Wilde.

Van Waters, Miriam. *Youth in Conflict.* New Republic.

Wembridge, Eleanor R. *Other People's Daughters.* Houghton Mifflin.

APPENDIX I

A CONSTITUTION FOR A YOUNG PEOPLE'S DEPARTMENT

Article I — *Name*

This organization shall be called the High School Department of the Church School.

Article II — *Object*

The object of this organization shall be (1) the study of God's word; (2) the promotion of friendship among its members; (3) an opportunity for expression through its activities; (4) training for Christian leadership.

Article III — *Membership*

Membership in this organization shall be open to pupils of classes in the High School Department of the Church School.

Article IV — *Dues*

There shall be no regular dues, but voluntary offerings may be called for and money may be earned through group activities whenever deemed advisable by the organization.

Article V — *Meetings*

Regular meetings shall be held every Sunday at noon and every Sunday evening at 6.30, preceded by a supper at 6 o'clock unless otherwise voted by the organization. Socials shall be held the fourth Friday of the month.

Article VI — *Council*

The Council shall be composed of one member from each class elected by the class. The pastor, director of religious education, department superintendent, and other department leaders desired by the council members shall be members *ex officio*. This group shall be the executive body of the department and shall meet the last Tuesday of every month. The Council shall have the power to ask any class to elect a new council member if the present member has failed to attend three consecutive council meetings without a good excuse and appears uninterested in the work of the organization. (If a young people's society exists, it may also elect representatives.)

Article VII — *Officers and Committees*

Section 1 — The officers of this organization shall be President, Vice-President, Secretary, and Treasurer; they shall be elected each year from the High School Council.

Section 2 — The committees shall be as follows: — Program, Supper, Membership, Social Service, Missionary, Social and any others that may from time to time be deemed advisable. The Chairmen shall be elected each year from the Council with the privilege of appointing their own committees.

Section 3 — The method of election shall be decided by the organization.

Article VIII — *Duties of Officers*

1. President — The President shall preside at all business meetings, be an *ex officio* member of all committees, and have general supervision of the expressional activities of the organization.

2. Vice-President — In the absence of the President, the Vice-President shall perform his duties.

3. Secretary — It shall be the duty of the Secretary to keep correct minutes of all business meetings of the organization and to have charge of correspondence pertaining to the organization.

4. Treasurer — It shall be the duty of the Treasurer to have charge of the finances of the expressional activities. He shall pay out only such sums as are voted by the Council.

Article IX — *Duties of Committees*

1. The Program Committee shall be responsible for the Sunday evening meetings, assigning programs to classes in the department.

2. The Supper Committee shall have charge of the Sunday evening suppers, assigning the serving of suppers to classes in the department.

3. The Membership Committee shall be on the lookout for new members and look up absentees.

4. The Social Service Committee shall plan and have charge of the Social Service program of the department.

APPENDIX II

DUTIES OF OFFICERS

The following questions are intended for the use of officers in helping them to check on themselves. It is suggested that they take that section which applies to them, and mark themselves on each of the ten questions. A person who feels that he measures up perfectly on each of them will mark himself 100; he will deduct from each possible score of 10 as much as he thinks represents his failure on that particular point. After each member has scored himself, it may be a wise plan for the executive committee to have a "truth meeting"; out of such a conference should come such constructive plans for improvement as the process of self-examination has revealed to be necessary.

President

1. Do I attend every meeting, "cutting" all other so-called important engagements? If I am compelled to be absent on account of sickness do I always notify the vice-president in plenty of time?

2. Do I regard this as one of the two or three most important activities in which I am engaged? Or do I "work at being president" only when I am not busy with something else?

3. Am I a leader or a boss? Do I have any trouble getting others to do their share of the work? If so, is it because I don't use the right method of approach?

4. Do I plan carefully just what I am going to do at a business meeting, just what I am going to say, and what I am going to do if things don't go the way that I hope they will?

5. Do I have regular meetings of the executive committee, dated so far ahead that there will be no excuse for making other engagements, and so well planned that members of the committee will regard the meetings as too important to miss?

6. How hard am I trying to keep up with what other groups are doing? When have I read a book on young people's work? Do I attend meetings where other leaders pass on suggestions of successful methods?

7. How hard am I trying to make my organization a real part of the working force of the church? Do I help along the idea that the young people's group is the " whole show "; or do I try to see that they " play the game " with the entire church?

8. As I look upon my work so far, is it going to be easy or hard for the next president to go on with the work when my term is up? How can I help to make it easier for him?

9. How often, in what ways, and with what kind of a spirit do I check up on all of the other officers? Do I always make sure that they are carrying out the instructions of the group, and that no details are left unattended to? Do I scold?

10. Am I careful to see that the definitely religious or spiritual side of our work is securing the central emphasis, or am I satisfied if our socials are a success and our members pay their dues? Where do I place the emphasis: upon good times or upon growing in Christian understanding and character?

Vice-President

1. Do I consider that I hold a very important office, or am I inclined to say, " Oh, the vice-president hasn't any particular responsibility " ?

2. Am I always present at all meetings? Do I consider that I am under the duty of being as regular in attendance as the president is?

3. Have I offered to relieve the president of some of the harder

parts of his job, such as checking up on details? If I have been trusted with this work have I taken it seriously?

4. Have I a single ounce of jealousy in me? Do I consider it an honor to be second in the list of officers, or do I have a feeling that "I could do it better than the president does"? What about my general attitude?

5. Do I work just as hard as if I were president? As I expect the present president to work?

6. Am I always ahead of time at the meetings, so that I may assume the leadership if the president does not arrive or is delayed?

7. Where am I placing the main emphasis: is the definitely religious or spiritual work of the group my main concern?

8. Am I efficient without being officious, able to get things done without bossing others?

9. At executive committee meetings do I try to support the president (except in cases when he seems to be clearly wrong), or do I insist upon my own opinions and thus make his work harder?

10. Suppose I were president and were working at that task in just the spirit that I am doing my duty as vice-president, would our organization have the kind of leader it needs? That is, am I showing my qualification for leadership by being both a good leader and a good follower?

Secretary

1. Am I "all there" at every meeting, giving careful attention to every word that is spoken? This is essential for a successful secretary.

2. Do I take down every action carefully, asking questions when I am in doubt about words, phrases and ideas?

3. Do I copy the notes of the meeting as soon as possible after getting home, before the notes "get cold" and I forget their meaning?

4. Do I keep my records as neatly as possible?

5. Do I keep the membership list alive, reporting to the proper committee the names of those who do not come and who should be looked up?

6. Do I record the names and addresses of strangers, for assignment to proper committees?

7. Do I look over the minutes before the next meeting, so that I am ready to suggest to the president any items of unfinished business which should be considered?

8. Do I keep the written reports of the chairman and officers systematically?

9. Do I take good care of the books and records which the retiring secretary hands on to me, and do I pass them on to my successor in as good condition — or better?

10. Do I notify promptly all persons appointed to regular or special committees? Is this notification in writing? Do I keep a record of when such notification was sent?

Treasurer

1. Do I count all money received in the collection in the presence of the secretary or some other person, making a public report of the total?

2. Do I keep a careful record of all dues paid, and notify the collector (unless that is also my duty) of those who are in arrears? In attempting to collect back dues do I combine a businesslike procedure with good nature?

3. Do I pay all bills promptly when authorized, paying no bills whatever without the proper instruction from the executive committee or other responsible persons?

4. Am I very careful never to borrow a cent from the treasury of the group for my own personal use? Am I sure that I never make an exception in this matter?

5. Do I keep my books as carefully as if I were the cashier of a bank?

6. Do I keep the money in a bank? If there is enough it should be kept in a checking account, all bills being paid by check and the stubs carefully saved.

7. Do I make regular reports, finding out from some capable adult just exactly how businesslike reports should be made?

8. Do I have my books examined at least twice a year by the executive committee, an auditing committee, or some person appointed to do it? This will save worry later if a mistake should be found, or if some other system of bookkeeping is needed.

9. Do I regularly compare the receipts and expenditures with the budget? If the expenses are running ahead of the amount agreed upon in the budget, do I take the matter up with the executive committee before paying such bills?

10. Do I keep my records in a safe place, carefully arranged and filed?

Chairmen of Committees

1. Do I realize that I have been selected as chairman of a given committee because it is believed that I have some ability for this task and because it is thought that I will be faithful in it? Have I made good on the expectations of the group?

2. Do I do my work with the same thoroughness that I expect of the president of the organization?

3. Am I present at all executive committee meetings; am I prompt; do I present carefully worked out reports in written form?

4. Do I consult with the president before deciding upon important plans, so that my committee will do nothing which is out of harmony with the general program of the group?

5. Do I hold regular meetings of my committee, with a businesslike procedure, and with definite subjects to discuss? Do I plan this in advance?

6. Do I see that my committee members work? It may be less trouble to do the work myself, but it is my duty to train the com-

mittee members by having them share the responsibility even though I have to spend time in checking up on them.

7. Do I try to dominate the committee, or am I willing to follow their ideas rather than trying to make them follow mine?

8. Do I realize that my committee is only one of several, that it must work with other committees, being neither selfish nor independent in its program?

9. Do I follow the wise precedents of others years, at the same time trying constantly to improve upon what other chairmen before me have done?

10. Do I see to it that the spiritual motive — loyalty to Jesus and an attempt to make His will dominant in life — is behind everything we do, whether it is planning socials, or arranging Sunday meetings, or trying to gain new members?

APPENDIX III

SUGGESTIONS FOR A CURRICULUM

Units Which May Be Considered

The following list of problems or projects represents a summary of questions which young people have asked their leaders. They indicate something of the variety of subjects regarding which the church should furnish help. A local committee may make up a three- or six-year curriculum, on either the quarter or semester basis, using such problems as these as the units for study, and drawing upon such printed materials as have some relation to the subjects. The denominational and interdenominational agencies of religious education will supply a bibliography.

To build a code of ethics or morals necessary for Christian young people of today.

To discover just what the religion of Jesus is.

To try to decide what a Christian should believe today.

To face the question of the effect of science upon religious beliefs and practices.

To understand the meaning of prayer and worship, and to build an organized practice of prayer and worship, individually and for the group.

To determine what should be the right attitude toward custom and habits.

To make a wise budget of time.

To determine the right use of money.

To establish wholesome relationships between the older and younger generations.

To understand the relations which should exist between the

sexes and to build the right type of social life between boys and girls.

To decide the right choice of a life work.

To study the principles which should guide one in the choice of a life partner.

To consider the matter of further education: what kind, how much, where?

To understand the program of the church and to share in its activities.

To study the program of modern missions and to assume such a share as seems right.

To understand the question, "Why do we have denominations?" and to build programs which will secure a larger interdenominationalism.

To understand the other religions of the world and to face the question of our duty toward them.

To study, "What great social problems will our generation be called upon to solve?" and to plan to assume the duties of Christian citizens.

To face the question of what responsibilities we have toward other races, far and near.

To understand what it means to be a patriot.

To discover what young people can do to get rid of war.

To study how to develop a program of Christian recreation.

Courses Based Largely upon Textbooks

The following recommendations are based largely on two considerations: interests apparent at the various age groups, and textbooks which are of special value.

Intermediate

Hunting: *Story of Our Bible* (Scribner's), 4 quarters

Hunting: *Religion in Everyday Life* (Pilgrim Press), 4 quarters

Buck: *Out of Their Own Mouths* (Abingdon Press), 1 quarter
Lobingier: *Our Church* (University of Chicago Press), 2 quarters
Sailer: *What Does Christ Expect of Young People Today?* (Pilgrim Press) 1 quarter

Senior

Stock: *Problems of Christian Youth* (Pilgrim Press), 1 quarter
Weston: *Jesus and the Problems of Life* (Pilgrim Press), 1 quarter
Weston: *Jesus' Teachings* (Pilgrim Press), 1 quarter
Stock: *Christian Life Problems* (Pilgrim Press), 1 quarter
Hill: *An Everyday Christian* (Abingdon Press), 1 quarter
Hill: *Christianity for Today* (Abingdon Press), 1 quarter
Lobingier: *Youth and the World Outlook* (Pilgrim Press), 1 quarter
Shaver: *A Christian's Patriotism* (University of Chicago Press), 1 quarter
Farmer: *The Christian Citizen and the Social and Industrial Problems of Today* (Westminster Press), 1 quarter
Kent: *The Social Teachings of the Prophets and Jesus* (Scribner's), 1 quarter
Reid: *Making Life Count* (Methodist Book Concern), 1 quarter (boys)
Moxcey: *Finding My Place* (Abingdon Press), 1 quarter (girls)
Thurston: *The Adventure of Prayer* (Revell), 1 quarter

Young People

Weston: *Problems and Principles of Social Living* (Pilgrim Press), Course XII, 1 quarter
Weston: *The World and Its Problems* (Pilgrim Press), 1 quarter
Soper: *What May I Believe?* (Abingdon Press), 1 quarter
Wembridge: *Other People's Daughters* (Houghton Mifflin), 1 quarter

Drake: *The New Morality* (Macmillan), 2 quarters

Robinson: *The Life of Paul* (University of Chicago Press), 2 quarters

Hayes: *Great Characters of the New Testament* (Abingdon Press), 1 quarter

Brown: *The Larger Faith* (Pilgrim Press), 1 quarter

Shaver: *Christian World-Builders* (University of Chicago Press), 1 quarter

Shaver: *A Christian's Recreation* (University of Chicago Press), 1 quarter

Fiske: *Jesus' Ideals of Living* (Abingdon Press), 2 quarters

Soper: *Faiths of Mankind* (Association Press), 1 quarter

Hawley: *The Teaching of the Old Testament* (Association Press), 1 quarter

Goodspeed: *The Story of the New Testament* (University of Chicago Press), 1 quarter

Winchester and Shaver: *The Teaching Church* (Pilgrim Press), 1 quarter

Gilkey: *A Faith for the New Generation* (Macmillan), 1 quarter

A current missionary text, recommended by the Missionary Education Movement, 1 quarter

A course on home-making, 2 quarters

A course on current social issues, 2 quarters

APPENDIX IV

COÖPERATIVE ACTIVITIES

The following activities may be carried on coöperatively by the young people of the various churches within a community, to the advantage of the religious life of all.

The Autumn Program

A survey of the community, to discover what young people are not being reached by the churches. The church preferences of all such should be stated and reported to the leaders of the several churches.

A rally program, which lasts longer than a single Sunday, and which includes distinctive worship sessions and worthy service objectives. Each church should make its own program, although all may agree to emphasize certain common elements. The publicity should be in the name of all the churches, although special invitations will go out to the constituency of each group.

A community Hallowe'en party given by the churches unitedly. This can become the biggest event in the community.

An Armistice commemoration which would have the distinctly Christian emphasis, and which might involve some phase of study and service as a part of the program in each local church.

A Fathers' and Sons' banquet, with community features, running throughout an entire week. Some of these events would be large mass occasions, others would center in the individual churches.

A Thanksgiving project, which would involve acts of service and friendship for the unfortunate. This would require a study of who should be helped, what kind of assistance would be most worth while, a plan of individual giving, the collection and preparation of baskets and of other provisions, the distribution to those who need it. It should be followed up with some method of continued friendship.

A similar Christmas project, with such other common features of the Christmas program as: the singing of Christmas carols, a community Christmas tree, a great young people's Christmas service, held at some time after each church has had its own Christmas worship or entertainment.

A watch-night service, which would include a banquet, social features, a rich worship service, and a young people's communion service (if the denominations agree that this is a wise plan).

The Mid-Winter Program

A go-to-church emphasis, with joint advertising, and united planning of common features. A mass meeting for young people might start the campaign.

A training school for leaders, or some type of institute, where the emphasis would be methodological, missionary, or along the lines of "personal enrichment."

A great Valentine party.

A series of programs which would center around the birthdays of national heroes.

A joint observance of Lent. Certain of the features would need to be reserved for the individual churches, such as the pastor's class; but there could be a common emphasis upon the value of joining the church, upon vesper services at which competent leaders would address young people upon the more spiritual aspects of religion, and upon such common gatherings as a Good Friday program, or a sunrise Easter service.

The Spring Program

A common endeavor to avoid the " after Easter slump."

A united plan by which young people will be helped to make a wise choice of their life work.

A joint endeavor to interest the local constituencies in the selection of capable young people as delegates to the approved summer conferences.

A common observance of Mothers' and Daughters' Week.

A joint welcome home to the students from college, particularly to those who have graduated and who are now expected to assume leadership in the local churches.

A project which centers around Goodwill Sunday.

The Summer Program

Joint sessions of the Sunday evening groups.

Outdoor and vesper services conducted by the young people jointly.

A method of welcoming visitors in the community to the church services.

A union picnic.

Providing a picnic for the old people of the community.

Arranging a method by which on a given day of each week the young people will take care of little children and give their mothers that opportunity to enjoy a needed freedom.

Giving a party or picnic for the juniors.

Coöperating in the establishment and conduct of vacation schools of religion.

INDEX